RECORDED VERSIONS
GUITAR
AUTHENTIC TRANSCRIPTIONS
WITH NOTES AND TABLATURE

BEST OF
MOTION CITY SOUNDTRACK

T0078797

Music transcriptions by Aurélien Budynek

ISBN 978-1-4234-8463-9

HAL•LEONARD®
CORPORATION
7777 W. BLUEMOUND RD. P.O. BOX 13819 MILWAUKEE, WI 53213

Visit Hal Leonard Online at
www.halleonard.com

from *Even If It Kills Me*

Broken Heart

Words and Music by Justin Pierre, Joshua Cain, Jesse Johnson, Matthew Taylor and Tony Thaxton

Tune down 1/2 step:
(low to high) Eb-Ab-Db-Gb-Bb-Eb

Verse
Fast ♩ = 156

2nd time, Gtr. 2: w/ Rhy. Fig. 2
2nd time, Gtrs. 3 & 4 tacet

*G   D/F#   Em

Riff A
Gtr. 1 (dist.)
mf
P.M.

1. I'll start __ this bro-ken heart, __ I'll fix it up __ so
2. I'll de-vise __ the best dis-guise, __ a brand new look and take __

*Chord symbols reflect implied harmony.

D   C   G/B

it will work __ a-gain __ bet-ter than __ be-fore. __
them by __ sur-prise, __ they'll nev-er guess __ what's not __

P.M.

2nd time, Gtr. 2: w/ Rhy. Fill 2

Gtr. 1: w/ Riff A

D5   G

__ in-side. __
__

Then I'll star __ in a
I'll ex-press my-self

End Riff A   Rhy. Fig. 1
Gtr. 2 (dist.)
mf
P.M.

P.M.

Rhy. Fill 2
Gtr. 2
P.M.

Copyright © 2007 Chrysalis Music and Hooray Let's Fight
All Rights Administered by Chrysalis Music
All Rights Reserved   Used by Permission

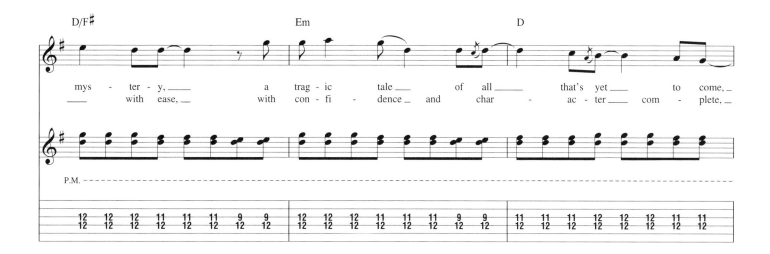

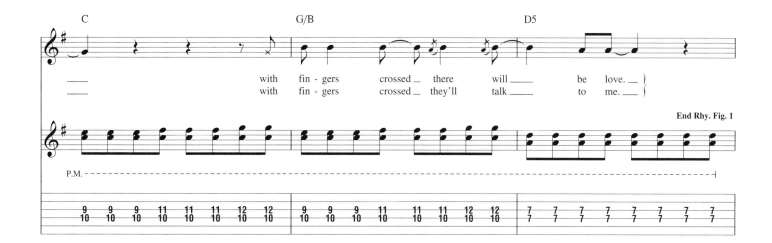

𝄋 Chorus

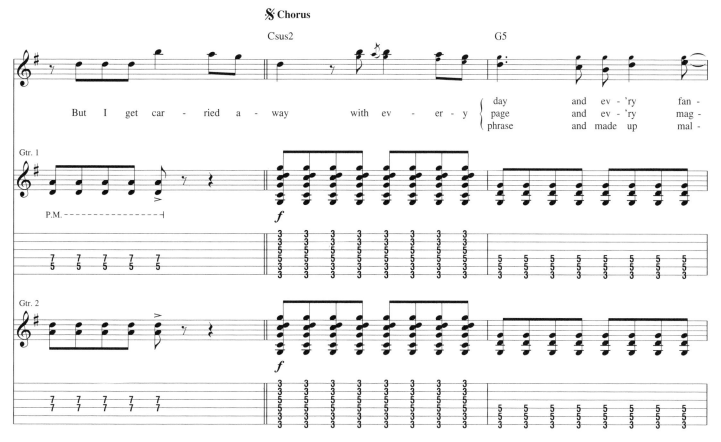

3

- ta - sy.___
- a - zine.___
- a - dy.___

The deep - er the wound the hard - er I
The cheap - er the thrill the deep - er I
The long - er I hide be - hind these

Gtrs. 1 & 2

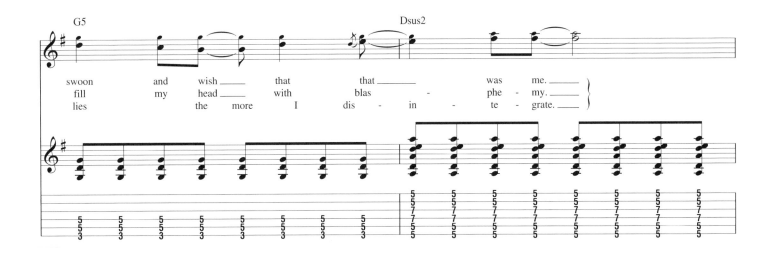

swoon and wish_____ that that_____ was me.___
fill my head_____ with blas - phe - my.___
lies the more I dis - in - te - grate.___

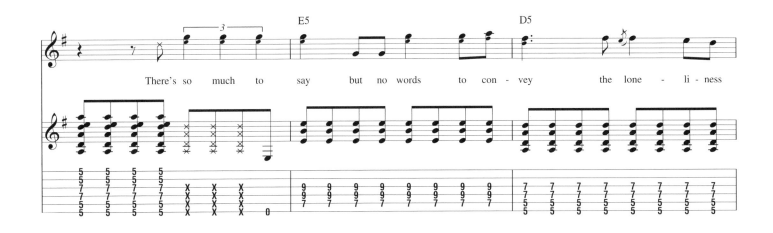

There's so much to say but no words to con - vey the lone - li - ness

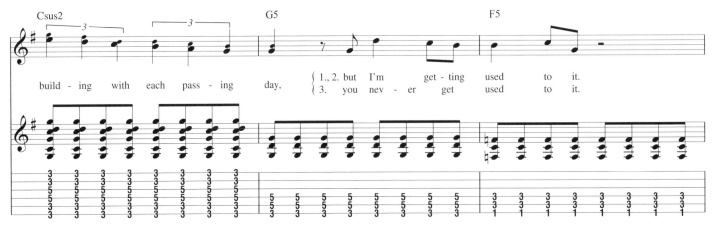

build - ing with each pass - ing day,
1., 2. but I'm get - ting used to it.
3. you nev - er get used to it.

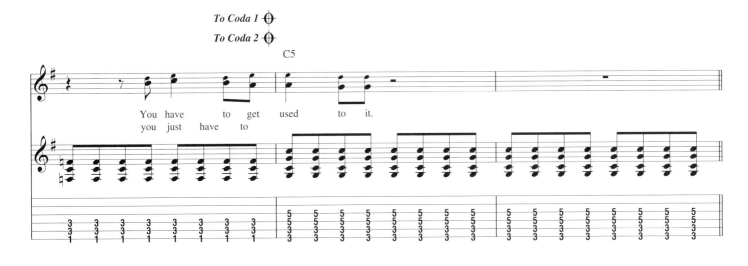

You have to get used to it.
you just have to

Interlude

Gtr. 1: w/ Riff A (1st 6 meas.)
Gtr. 2 tacet

G   D/F#   Em   D

D.C. al Coda 1

Gtr. 1: w/ Rhy. Fill 1

C   G/B   D5

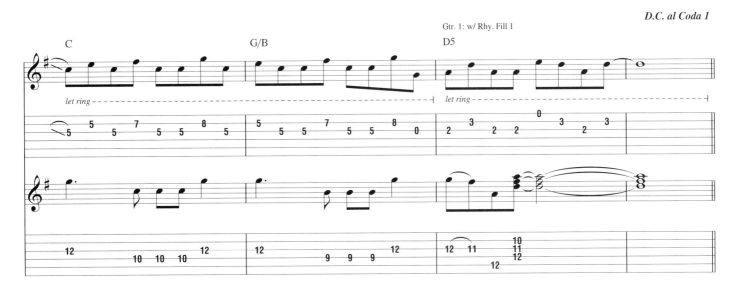

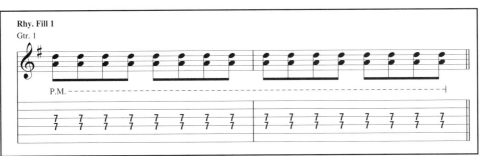

5

⊕ Coda 1

Synth Solo
Half-time feel

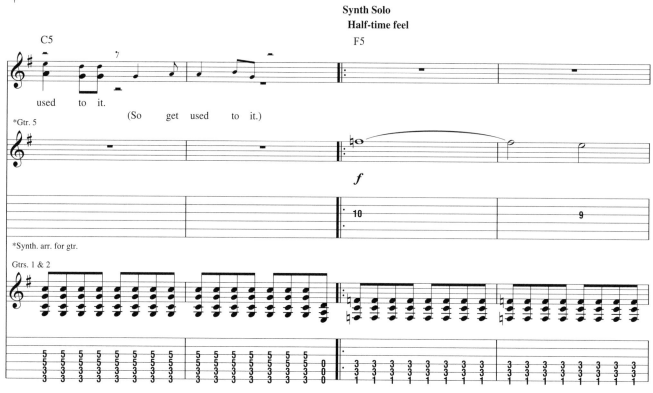

used to it.

(So get used to it.)

*Gtr. 5

*Synth. arr. for gtr.

Gtrs. 1 & 2

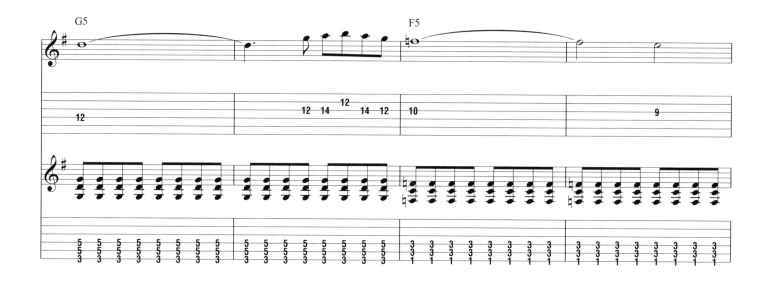

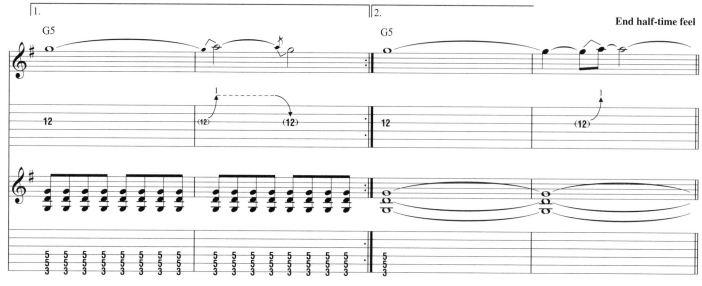

End half-time feel

Verse

Gtrs. 1, 2 & 5 tacet

3. I'll de-stroy _ this use-less heart, _ I'll fuck it up so it-'ll nev-er beat _ a - gain, _

*Chords implied by bass, next 7 meas.

D.S. al Coda 2

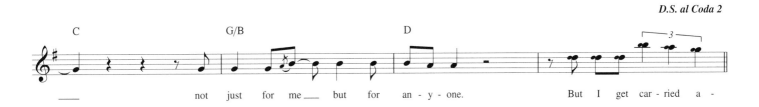

_ not just for me _ but for an - y - one. But I get car-ried a -

 Coda 2

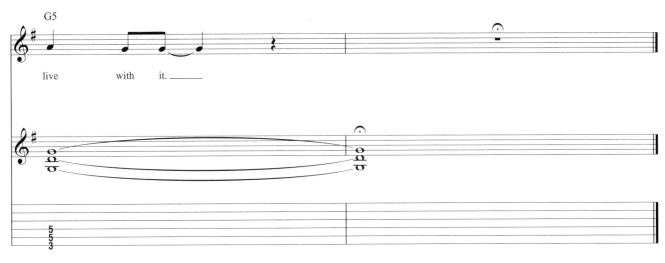

live with it. _____

Everything Is Alright

Words and Music by Justin Pierre, Joshua Cain, Jesse Johnson, Matthew Taylor and Tony Thaxton

Tune down 1/2 step:
(low to high) E♭-A♭-D♭-G♭-B♭-E♭

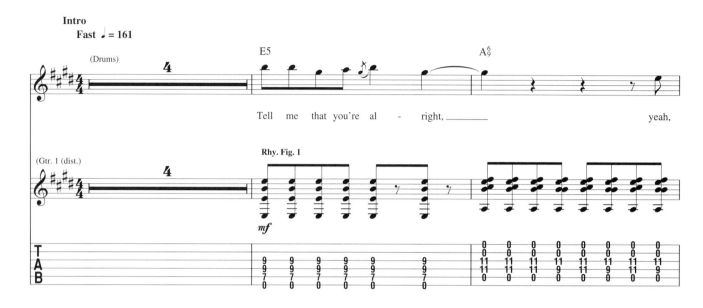

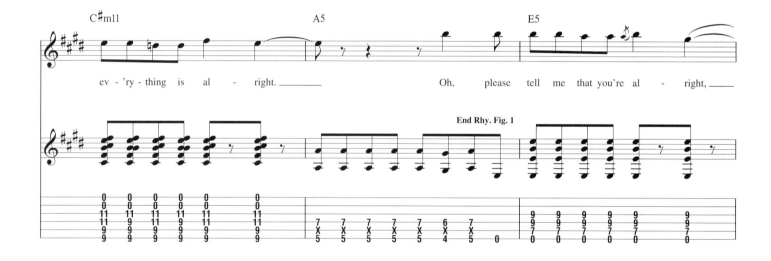

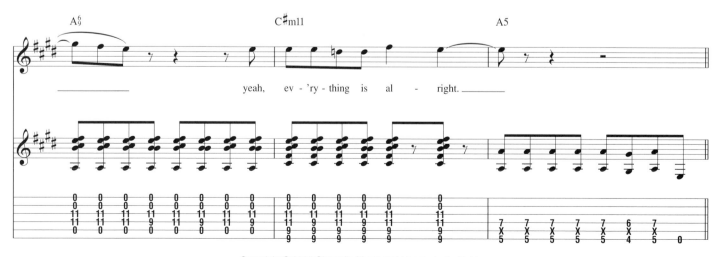

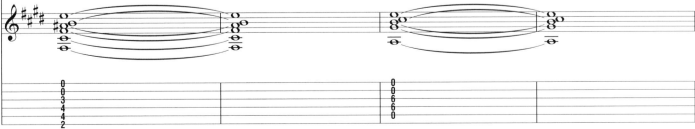

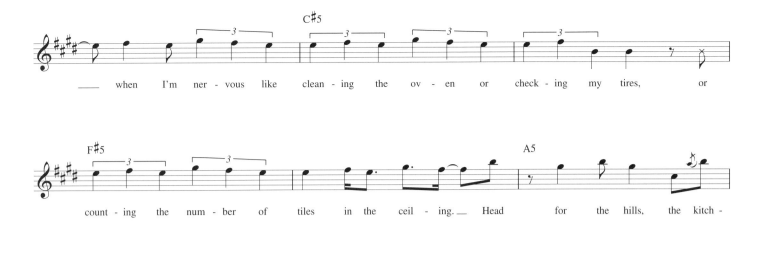

when I'm ner - vous like clean - ing the ov - en or check - ing my tires, or

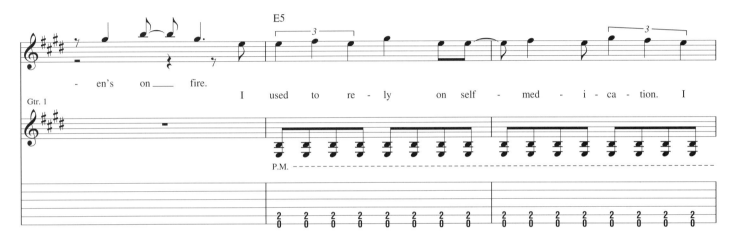

count - ing the num - ber of tiles in the ceil - ing. Head for the hills, the kitch -

- en's on ___ fire. I used to re - ly on self - med - i - ca - tion. I

Gtr. 1

P.M.

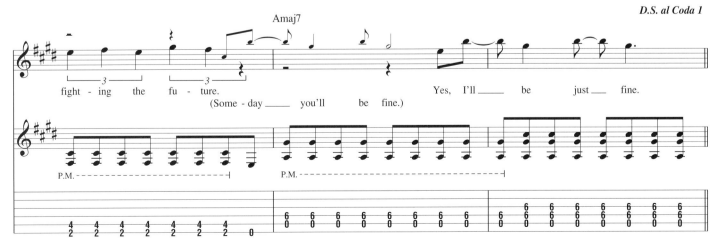

guess I still do that from ___ time to time. But I'm get - ting bet - ter at

P.M. P.M.

D.S. al Coda 1

fight - ing the fu - ture. Yes, I'll ___ be just ___ fine.
(Some - day ___ you'll be fine.)

P.M. P.M.

Coda 1

Interlude

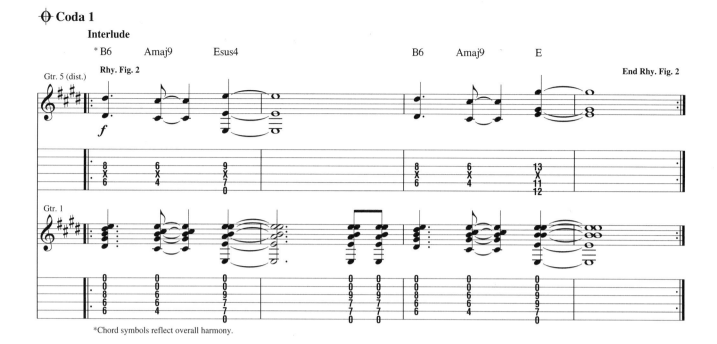

*Chord symbols reflect overall harmony.

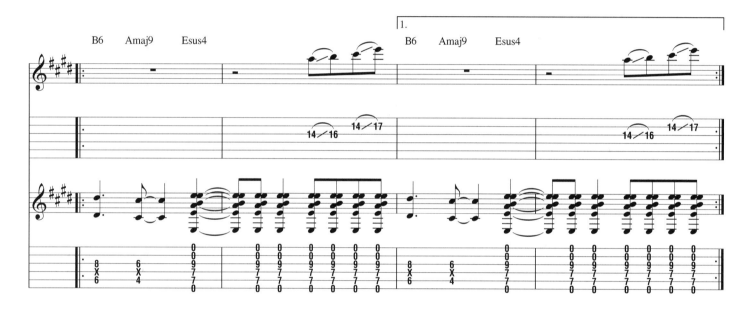

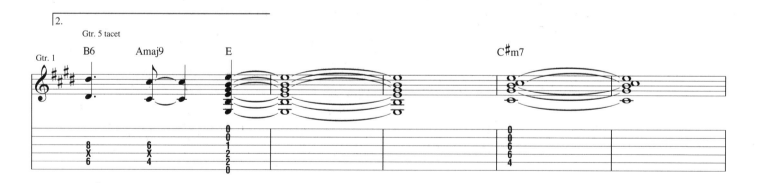

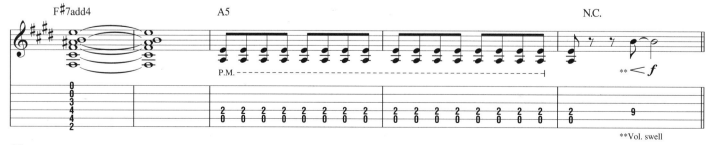

**Vol. swell

Bridge

Give me a rea - son, _____ to end ____ this dis - cus - sion _____ to break

(I don't be - lieve _ a word ____ of an - y - thing _ I've heard, __)

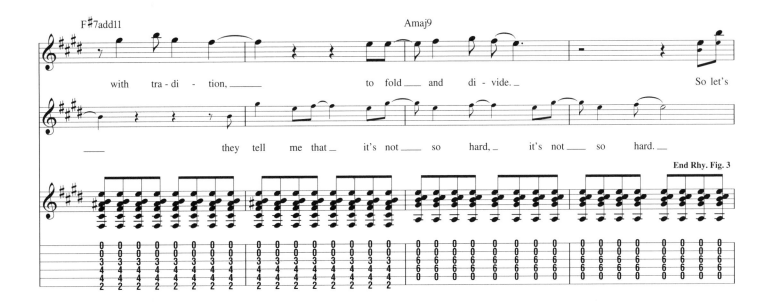

with tra - di - tion, _____ to fold ____ and di - vide. _ So let's

____ they tell me that __ it's not ____ so hard, _ it's not ____ so hard. _

Gtr. 1: w/ Rhy. Fig. 3

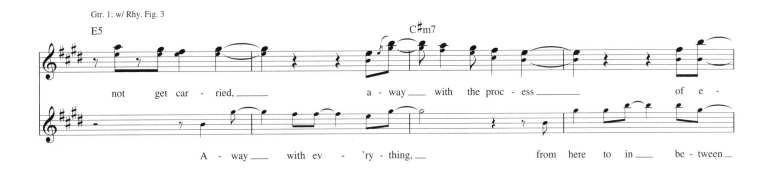

not get car - ried, _____ a - way ____ with the proc - ess _____ of e -

A - way ____ with ev - 'ry - thing, ___ from here to in ____ be - tween __

D.S. al Coda 2

- lim - i - na - tion, _____ I don't want ____ to waste ___ your time. ____

____ the long good - bye. I don't want ____ to waste ___ your time.) __

⊕ Coda 2

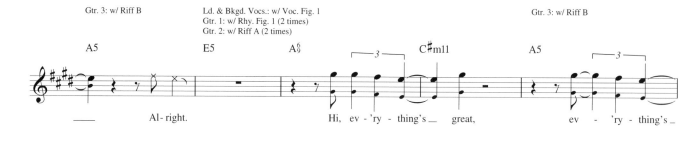

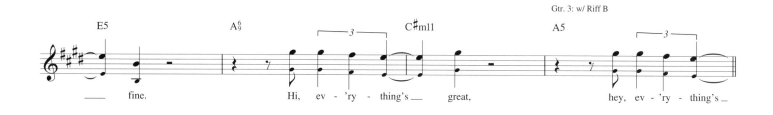

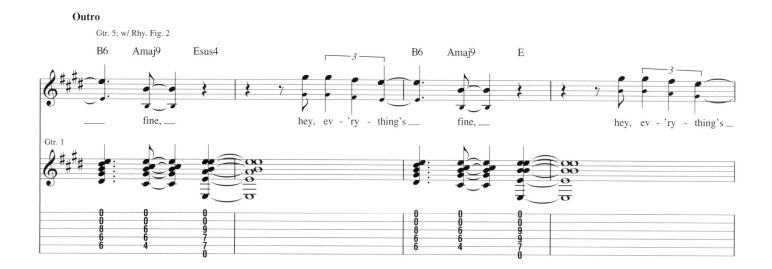

Outro

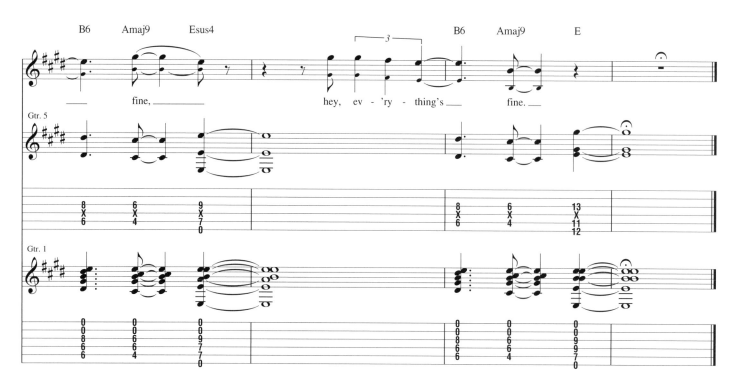

from *Even If It Kills Me*

Fell in Love Without You

Words and Music by Justin Pierre, Joshua Cain, Jesse Johnson, Matthew Taylor and Tony Thaxton

Tune down 1/2 step:
(low to high) E♭-A♭-D♭-G♭-B♭-E♭

Intro

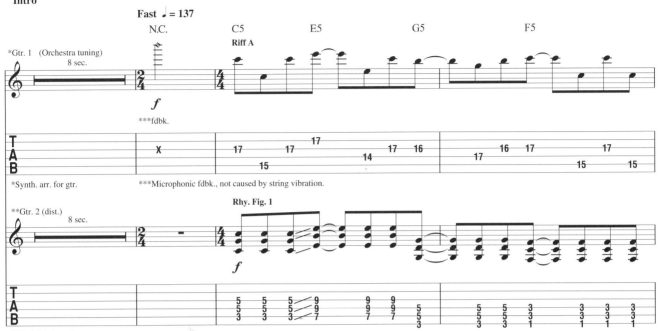

*Synth. arr. for gtr.   ***Microphonic fdbk., not caused by string vibration.

**Doubled throughout

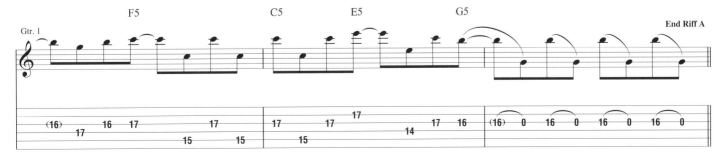

℅ Verse

Gtr. 1 tacet

*Chords implied by bass, next 7 meas.

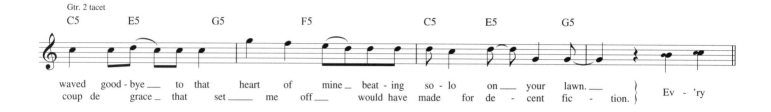

Chorus

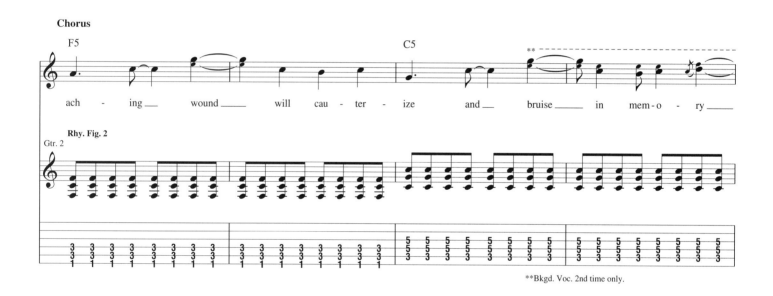

**Bkgd. Voc. 2nd time only.

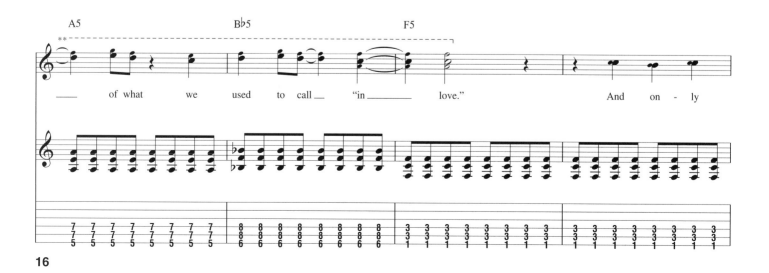

16

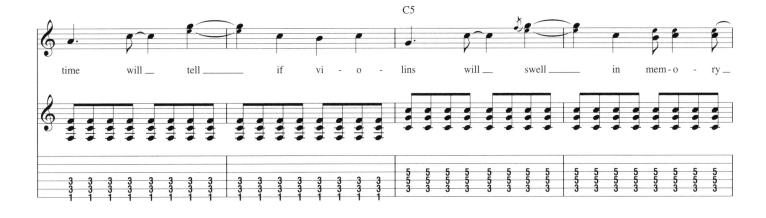

time will __ tell _____ if vi - o - lins will __ swell _____ in mem - o - ry __

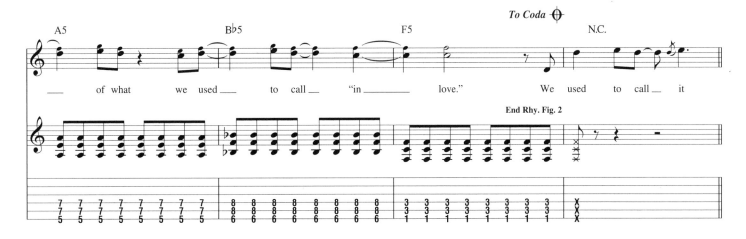

To Coda ⊕

__ of what we used ___ to call __ "in _____ love." We used to call __ it

End Rhy. Fig. 2

D.S. al Coda

Interlude

Gtr. 1: w/ Riff A
Gtr. 2: w/ Rhy. Fig. 1 (2 times)

"love." _____

⊕ **Coda**

Guitar Solo

Gtr. 2: w/ Rhy. Fig. 2

used to call ___ it...

Gtr. 3 (dist.)

Gtr. 2

Gtr. 1

*fdbk.

*Microphonic fdbk., not caused by string vibration.

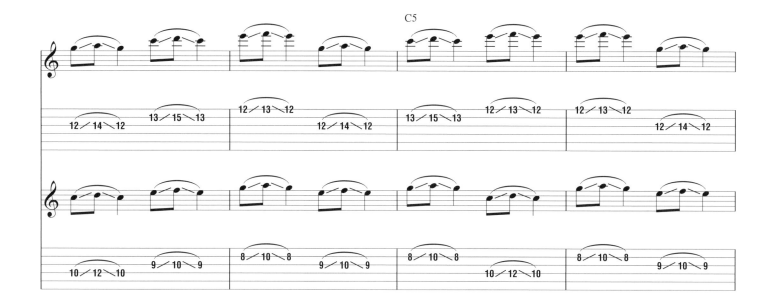

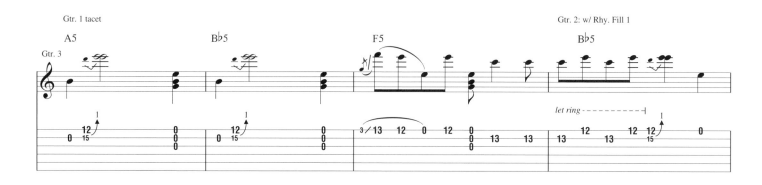

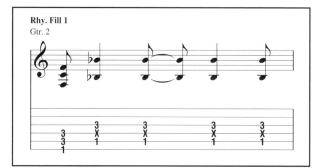

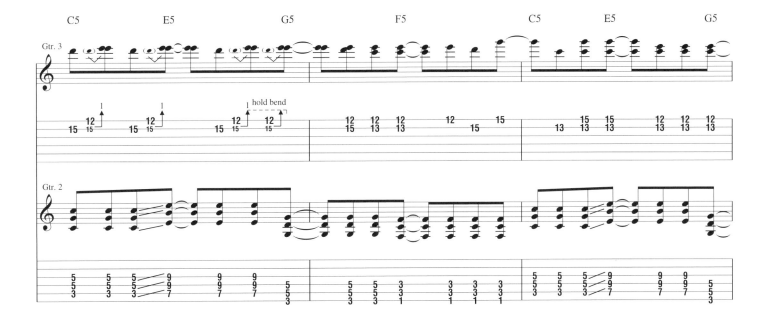

Verse

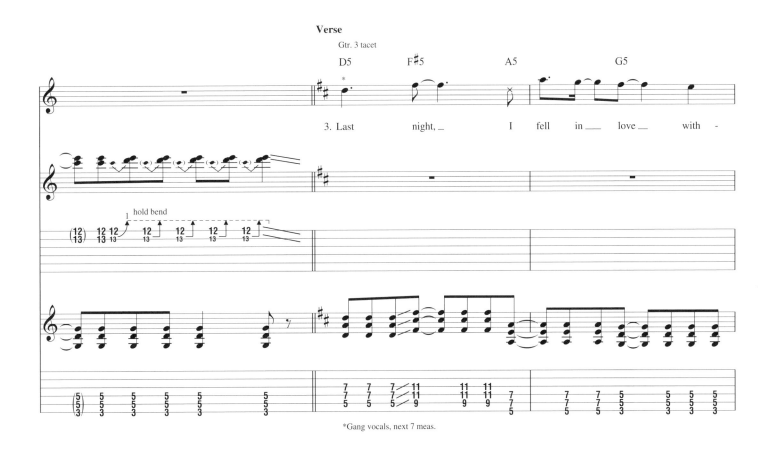

3. Last night, __ I fell in __ love __ with -

*Gang vocals, next 7 meas.

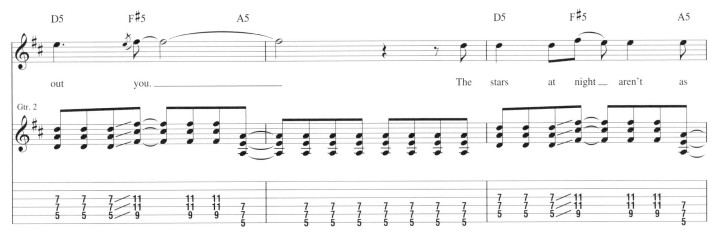

out you. __ The stars at night __ aren't as

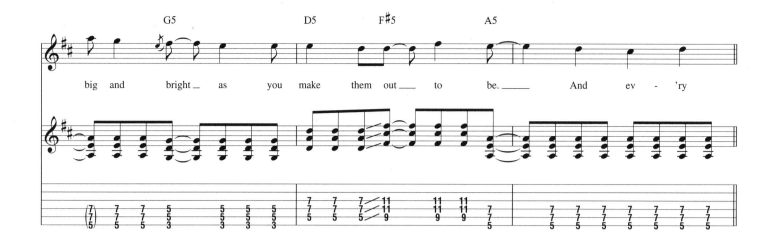

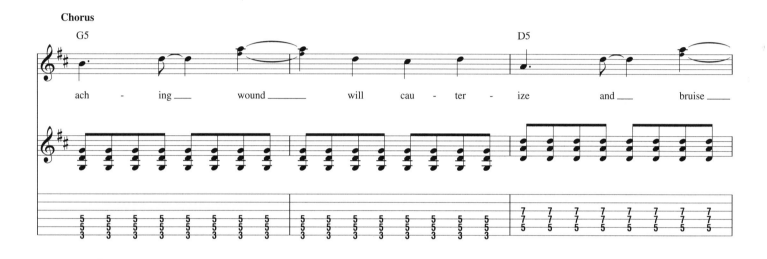

Chorus

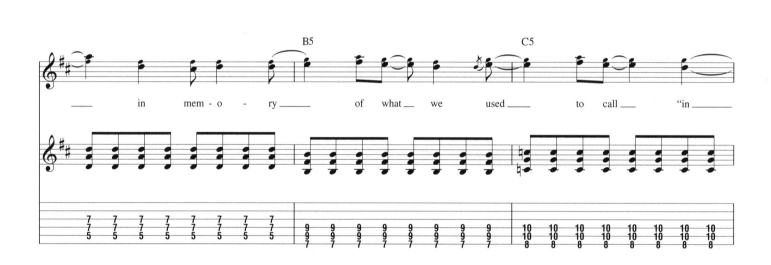

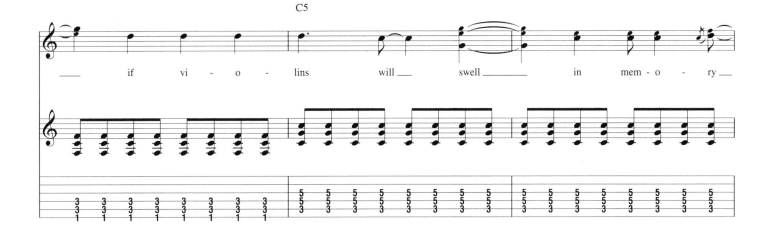

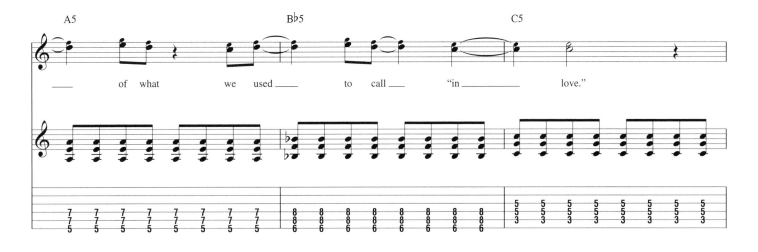

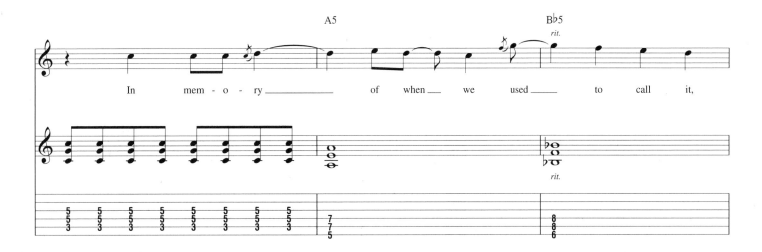

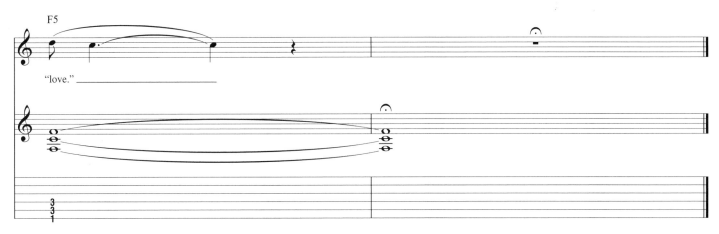

from *Even If It Kills Me* Acoustic EP

Fell in Love Without You (Acoustic)

Words and Music by Justin Pierre, Joshua Cain, Jesse Johnson, Matthew Taylor and Tony Thaxton

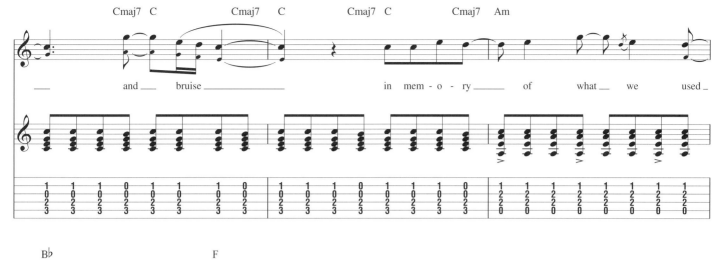

and ___ bruise ___ in mem - o - ry ___ of what ___ we used ___

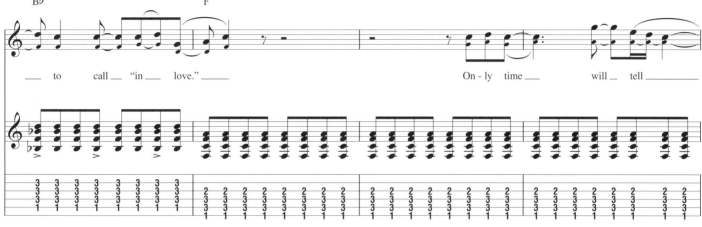

___ to call ___ "in love." ___ On - ly time ___ will ___ tell ___

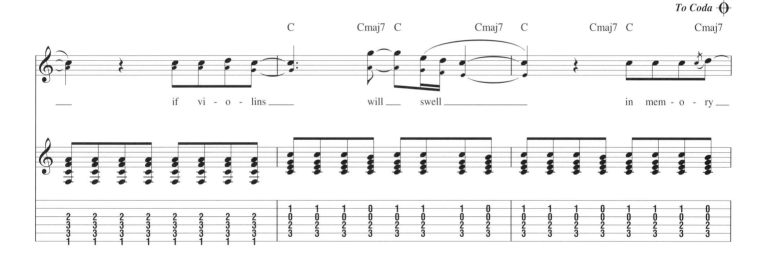

To Coda

___ if vi - o - lins ___ will ___ swell ___ in mem - o - ry ___

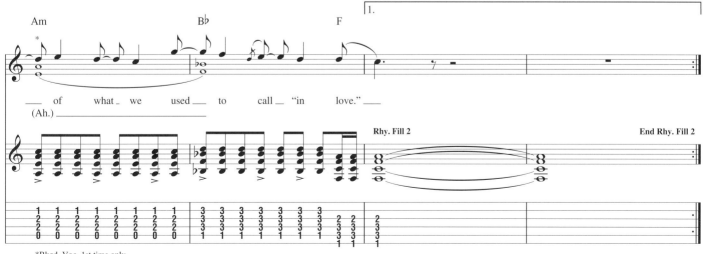

1.

___ of what ___ we used ___ to call ___ "in love." ___
(Ah.) ___

Rhy. Fill 2   End Rhy. Fill 2

*Bkgd. Voc. 1st time only.

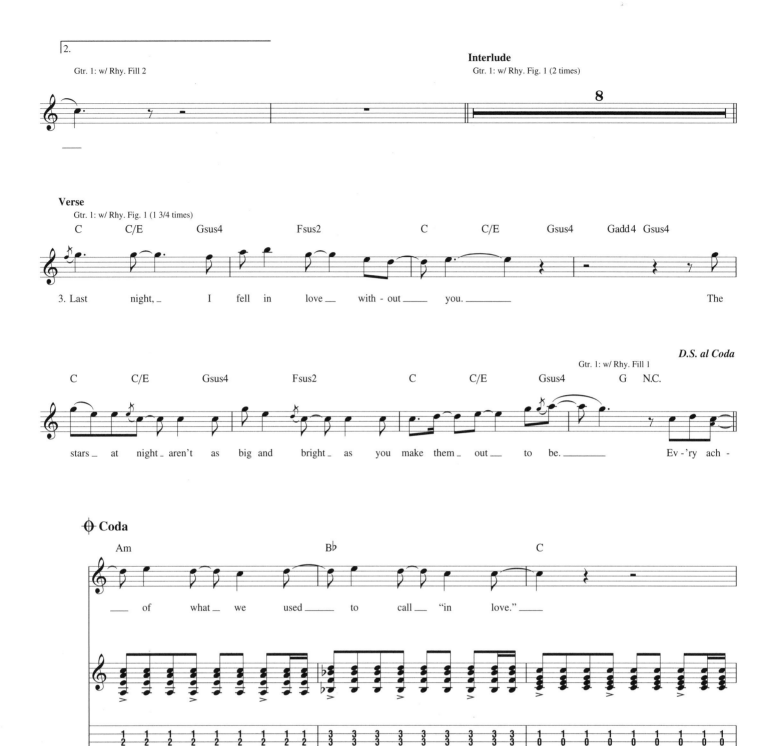

2.

Gtr. 1: w/ Rhy. Fill 2

Interlude

Gtr. 1: w/ Rhy. Fig. 1 (2 times)

8

Verse

Gtr. 1: w/ Rhy. Fig. 1 (1 3/4 times)

C   C/E   Gsus4   Fsus2   C   C/E   Gsus4   Gadd4 Gsus4

3. Last   night,   I   fell   in   love   with - out   you.   The

D.S. al Coda

Gtr. 1: w/ Rhy. Fill 1

C   C/E   Gsus4   Fsus2   C   C/E   Gsus4   G   N.C.

stars   at   night   aren't   as   big and   bright   as   you make them   out   to be.   Ev -'ry ach -

Coda

Am   B♭   C

     of   what   we   used   to   call   "in   love."

Am   *B♭   F

rit.

In mem-o - ry   of   what   we   used   to   call   "in   love."

rit.

*Final two chords played by piano.

24

from *I Am the Movie*

The Future Freaks Me Out

Words and Music by Justin Pierre, Joshua Cain, Jesse Johnson, Matthew Taylor and Tony Thaxton

Tune down 1/2 step:
(low to high) E♭-A♭-D♭-G♭-B♭-E♭

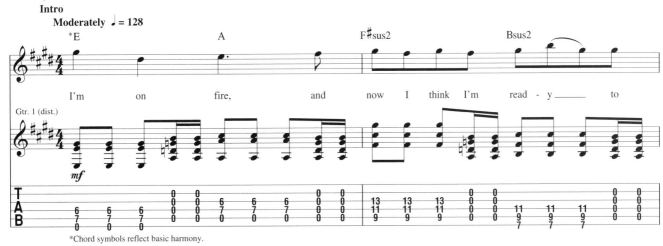

*Chord symbols reflect basic harmony.

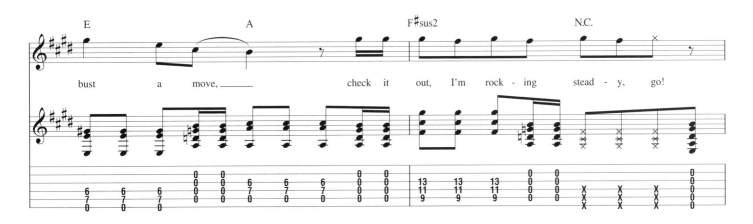

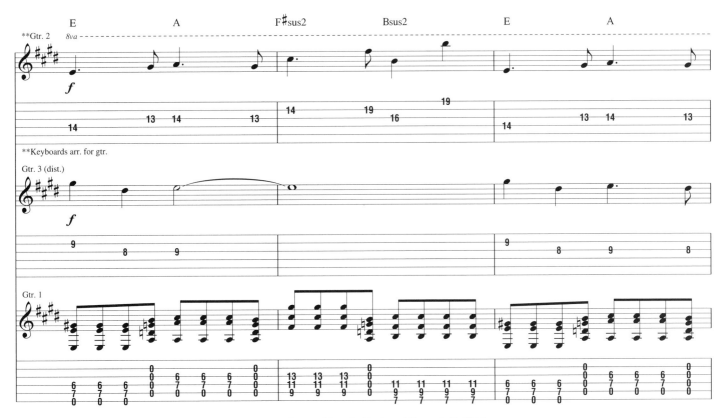

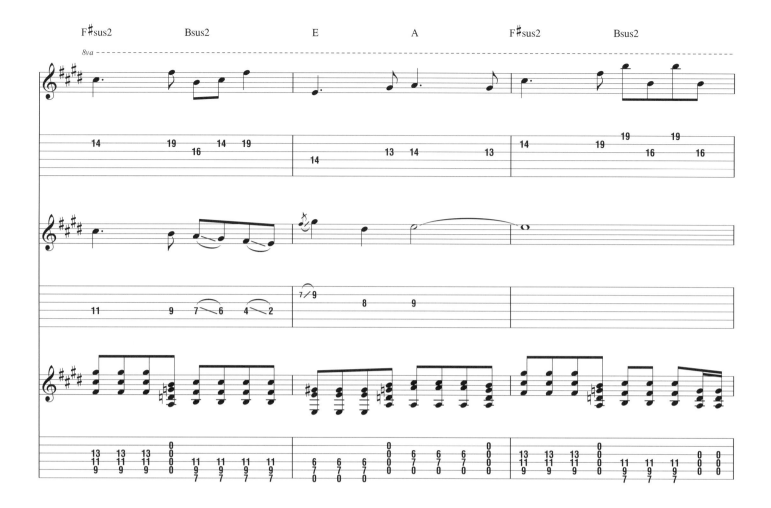

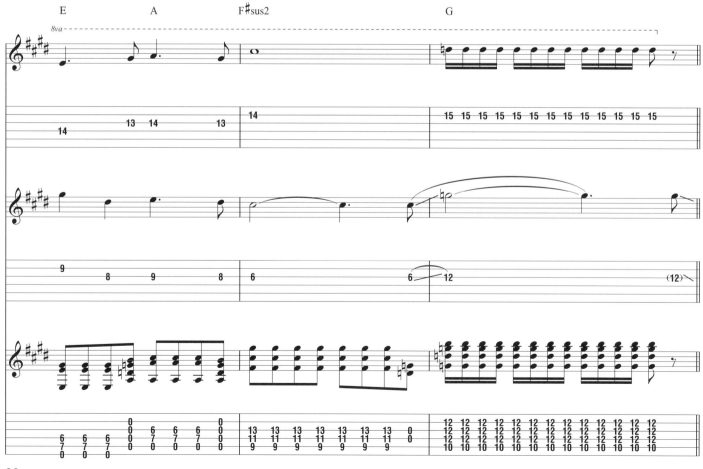

Verse

1. Bet - ty won't stop lis - ten - ing to mod - ern rock, how ___ she hates to be a - lone.

I try to com - pen - sate her lack of love with cof - fee cake, ice ___ cream and a bot - tle of ten

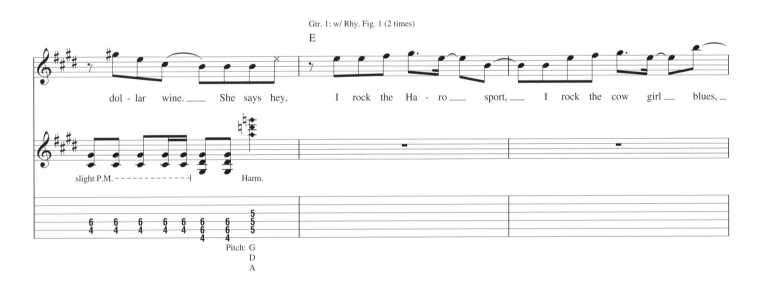

dol - lar wine. ___ She says hey, I rock the Ha - ro ___ sport, ___ I rock the cow girl ___ blues, ___

___ I rock too fast for love, I'm foot - loose in my Vel - cro ___ shoes. ___ What's up with Will and ___ Grace? ___

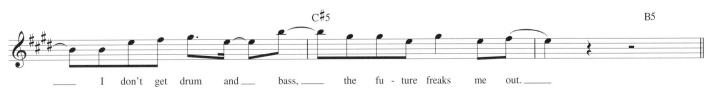

___ I don't get drum and ___ bass, ___ the fu - ture freaks me out. ___

27

Interlude

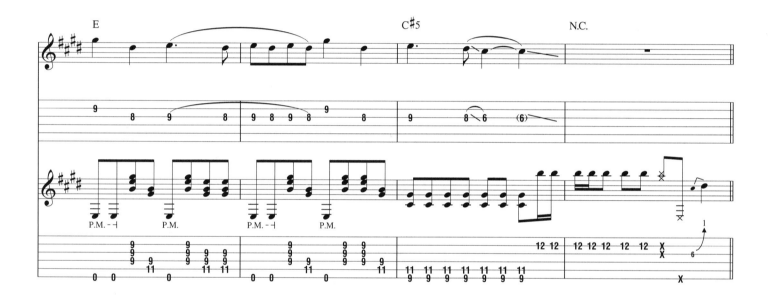

𝄋 Chorus

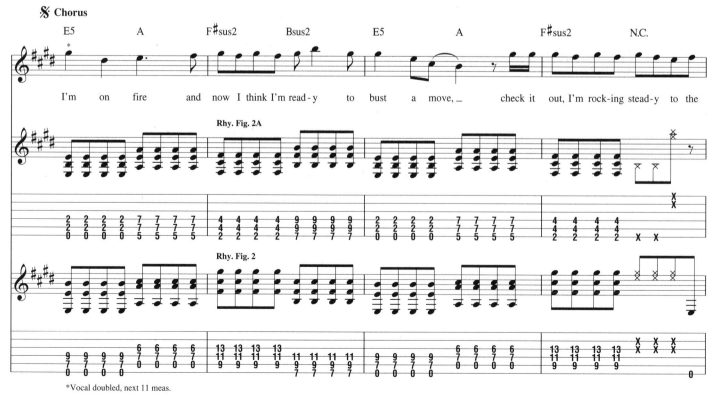

I'm on fire and now I think I'm read-y to bust a move,— check it out, I'm rock-ing stead-y to the

*Vocal doubled, next 11 meas.

28

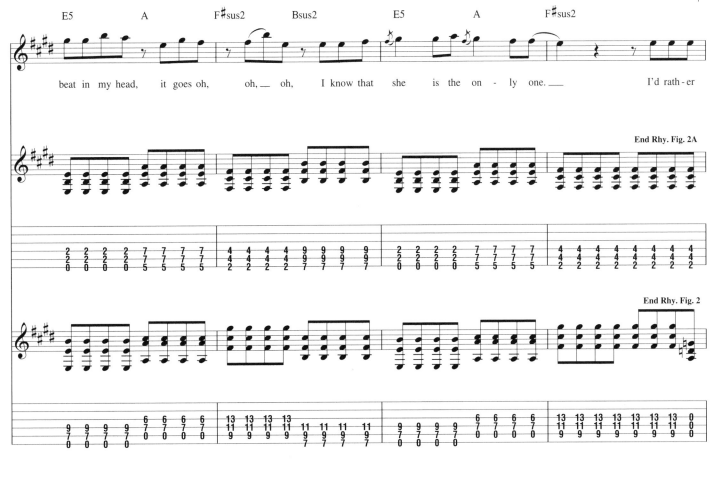

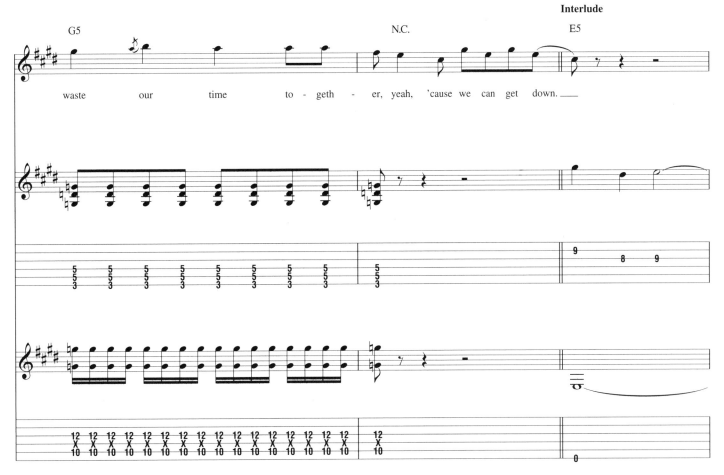

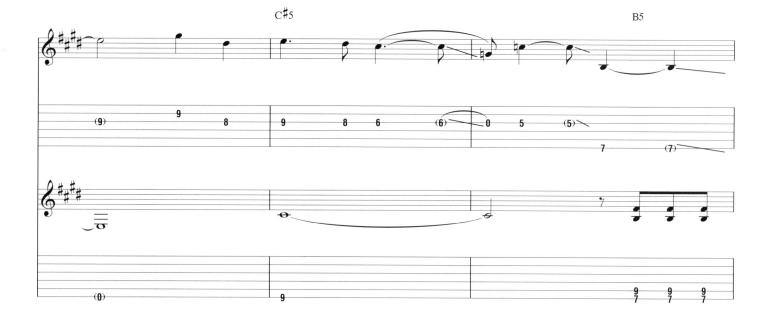

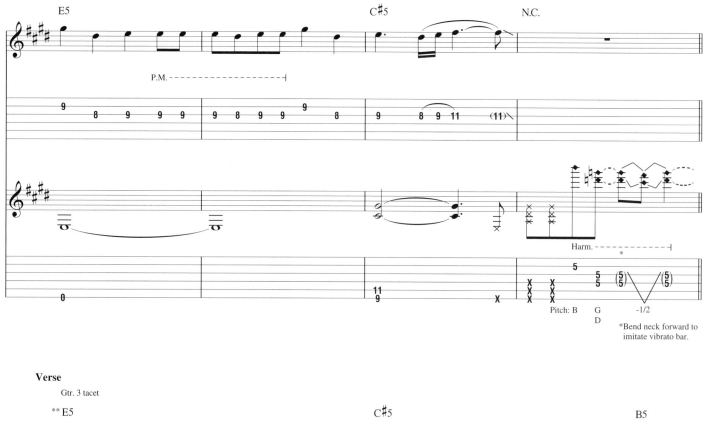

Verse

Gtr. 3 tacet

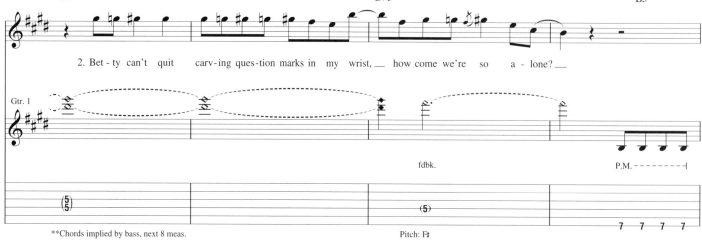

2. Bet-ty can't quit carv-ing ques-tion marks in my wrist,__ how come we're so a-lone?__

**Chords implied by bass, next 8 meas.

Pitch: F#

30

We waste a-way the days with nic-o-tine and tel-e-vi-sion sam - ples of an e-ra we hate

to ad-mit we em-brace. We fail to rep-re - sent, ___ we fail to be con-tent, ___

___ we fail at ev-'ry-thing we ev-er e-ven try to at-tempt. And so the sto-ry ___ goes, ___

D.S. al Coda

___ as on-ly Bet-ty ___ knows, ___ it's time to take con-trol. ___ Get down!

Coda

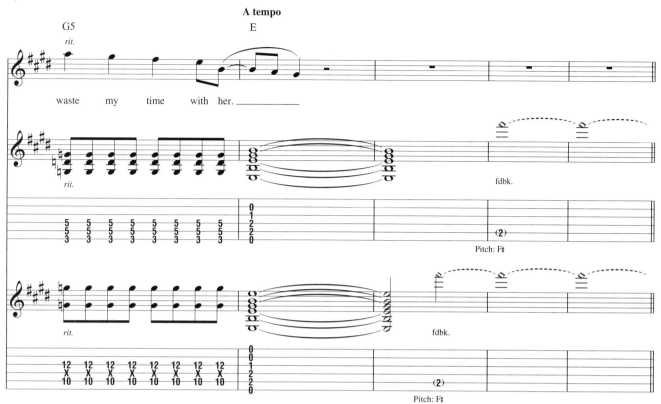

Bridge

*Bkgd. voc. doubled, next 19 meas.

out you to call up on the week-ends with my cel-lu-lar phone, ___ oh.

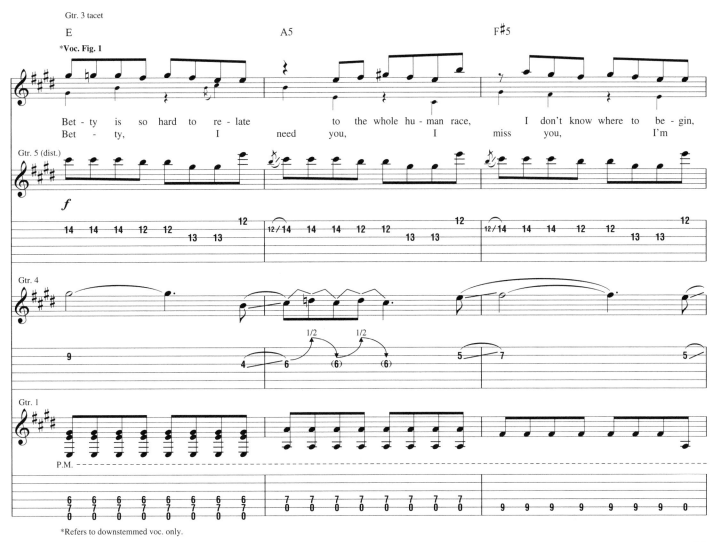

Bet-ty is so hard to re-late to the whole hu-man race, I don't know where to be-gin,
Bet - ty, I need you, I miss you, I'm

*Refers to downstemmed voc. only.

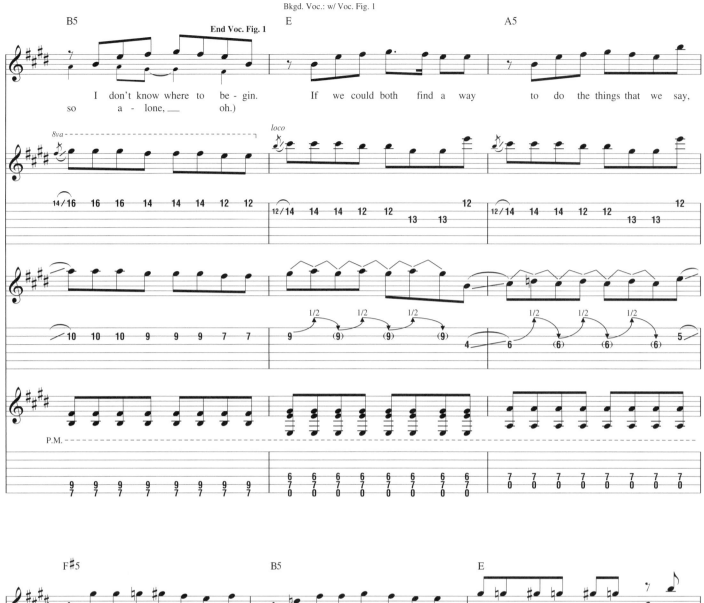

from *Commit This to Memory*

Hold Me Down

Words and Music by Justin Pierre, Joshua Cain, Jesse Johnson, Matthew Taylor and Tony Thaxton

*Chord symbols reflect implied harmony.

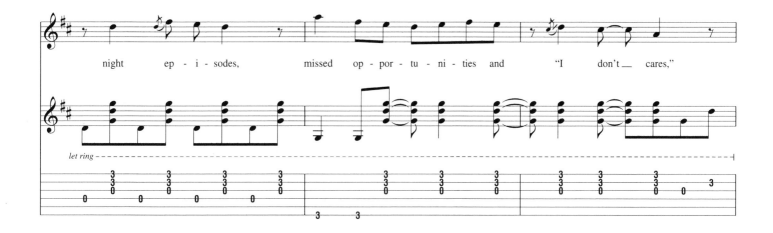

night ep - i - sodes, missed op - por - tu - ni - ties and "I don't __ cares,"

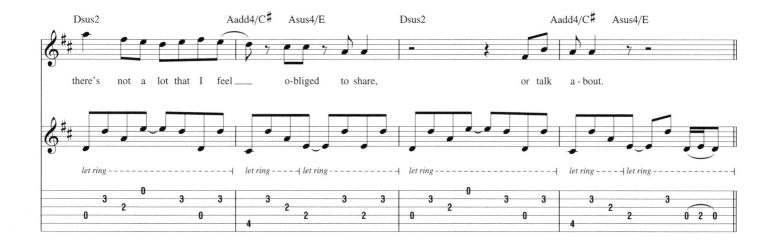

Dsus2   Aadd4/C#   Asus4/E   Dsus2   Aadd4/C#   Asus4/E

there's   not   a   lot   that   I   feel ___   o-bliged   to   share,   or   talk   a - bout.

Interlude

Gtr. 1: w/ Riff A

Dsus2   Asus4   Dsus2

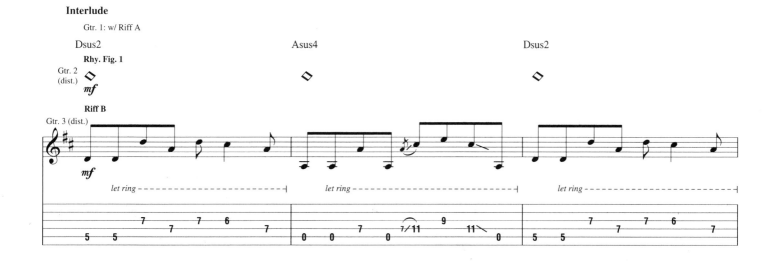

Asus4   Dsus2   Asus4

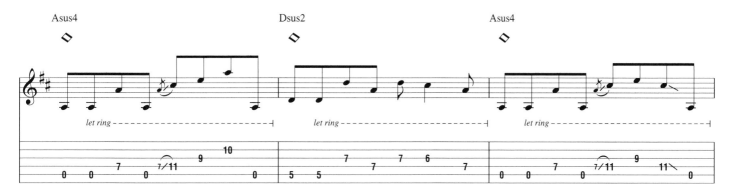

How will I break the news __ to you? __

Gtr. 3

*Vol. swell

Interlude

Gtr. 1: w/ Riff A
Gtrs. 2: w/ Rhy. Fig. 1
Gtr. 3: w/ Riff B

Dsus2   Asus4   Dsus2   Asus4   Asus4

1.   2.

Gtr. 4 (clean)

mf

Verse

Gtr. 1: w/ Riff A   Gtr. 4 tacet

D   A   D   A

3. Can - cel our din - ner with Max __ and Cor - a - line, feed Jack - y's ger - bil and try ___ to stay __ clean.

Gtr. 4

Gtr. 2

Gtr. 2
divisi   *let ring -*

D   A   D   A

We'll talk it o - ver af - ter ___ I've had __ some _____ time a - lone ___ to sort it out.

let ring -

Pre-Chorus

You hold me down, ___   you hold me down, ___   you hold me down, ___

Chorus

Bkgd. Voc.: w/ Voc. Fig. 1 (4 times)
Gtr. 1: w/ Rhy. Fig. 4 (4 times)

___   you hold me down. ___   You're the ech-oes of ___ my ev-'ry-thing, ___ you're the

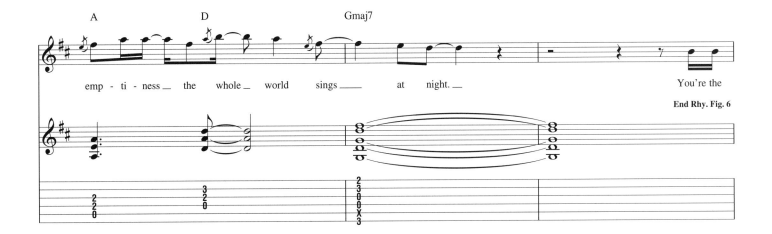

emp-ti-ness ___ the whole world sings ___ at night. ___   You're the

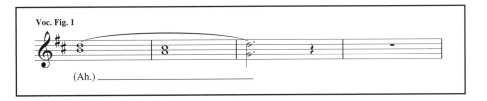

Voc. Fig. 1

(Ah.) ___

Gtr. 3 tacet

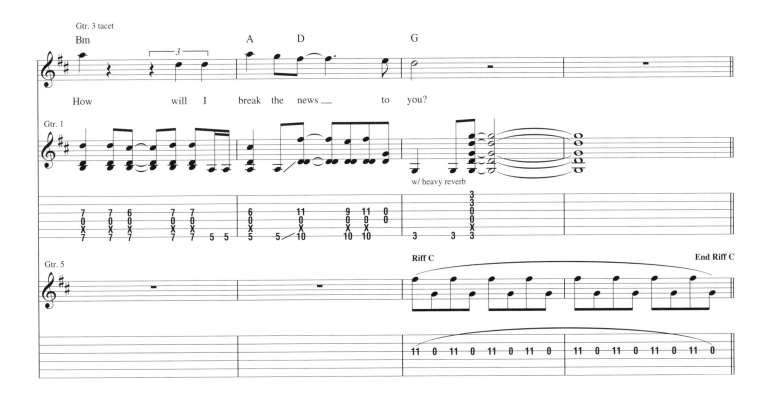

How will I break the news __ to you?

Gtr. 1

w/ heavy reverb

Gtr. 5

Riff C   End Riff C

Outro

*Gtr. 5: w/ Riff C (18 times)
Gtr. 1 tacet

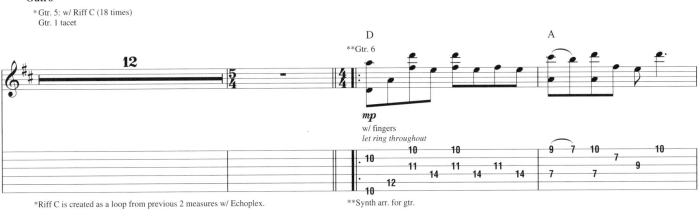

mp
w/ fingers
let ring throughout

*Riff C is created as a loop from previous 2 measures w/ Echoplex.

**Synth arr. for gtr.

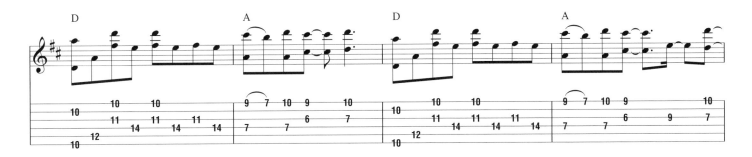

1., 2.   3.
                                         Gtr. 6 tacet

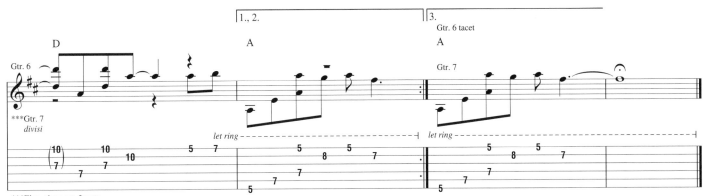

***Gtr. 7
divisi

let ring -   *let ring* -

***Elec. piano arr. for gtr.

from *Even If It Kills Me*

It Had to Be You

Words and Music by Justin Pierre, Joshua Cain, Jesse Johnson, Matthew Taylor and Tony Thaxton

Tune down 1/2 step:
(low to high) E♭-A♭-D♭-G♭-B♭-E♭

Intro
Moderately fast ♩ = 144
Fade in

*Esus2

Gtr. 1 (slight dist.)

*Chord symbols reflect implied harmony.

Verse

1. I ___ get lost, messed ___ up and bored ___ when I'm ___ a - lone ___ too long. ___

Riff A   **End Riff A**

Gtr. 1: w/ Riff A 1 (3 times)

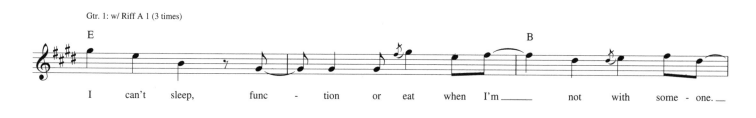

I can't sleep, func - tion or eat when I'm ___ not with some - one. ___

___ Late last fall she end - ed it all and moved ___

___ to who knows where. ___ Just like that she van -

-ished and packed and nev - er e - ven called.___ Do you feel a cer-

Pre-Chorus

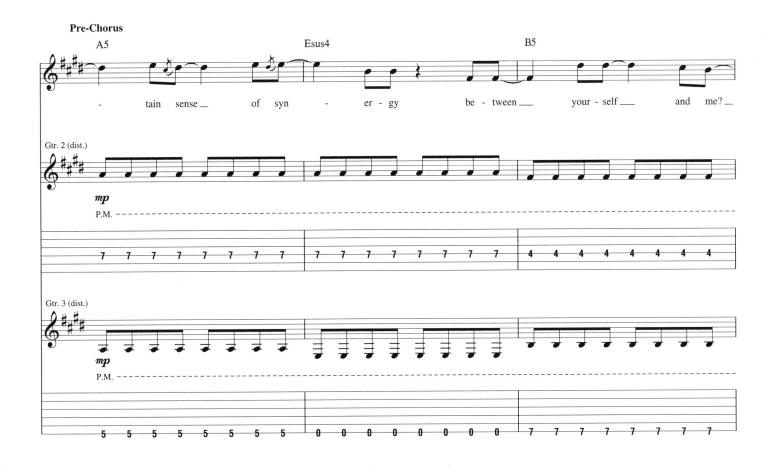

-tain sense ___ of syn - er - gy be - tween ___ your - self ___ and me? ___

Gtr. 2 (dist.)

mp

P.M. -

Gtr. 3 (dist.)

mp

P.M. -

___ A kind of ma - cabre ___ and som - ber won - der - twin type of

P.M. -

P.M. -

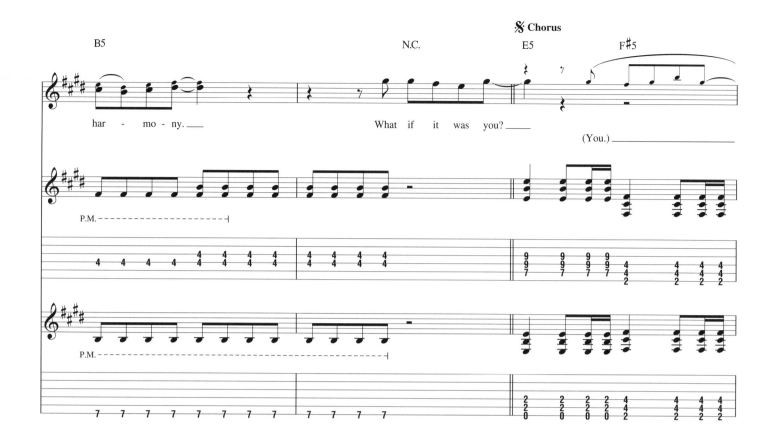

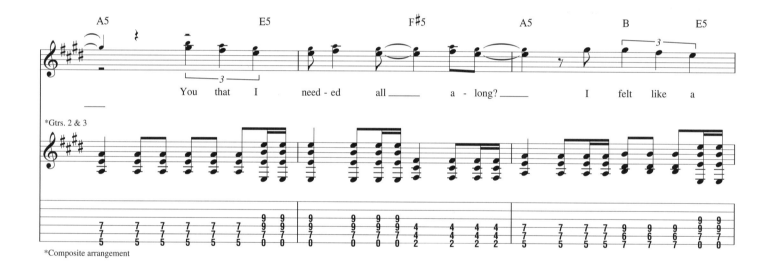

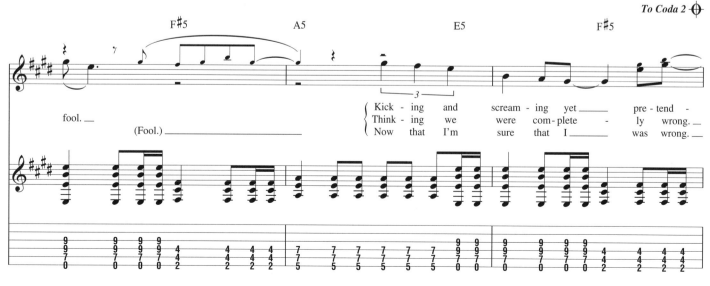

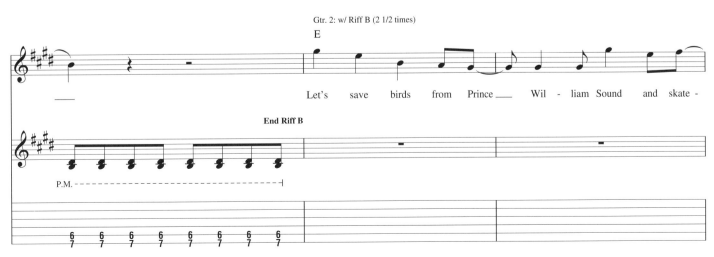

-board through __ the mall. __   Let's fight crime with man - gos and limes and join __

__ the P. __ G. A. __   Let's win big with ev - er - y spin but hur -

Pre-Chorus

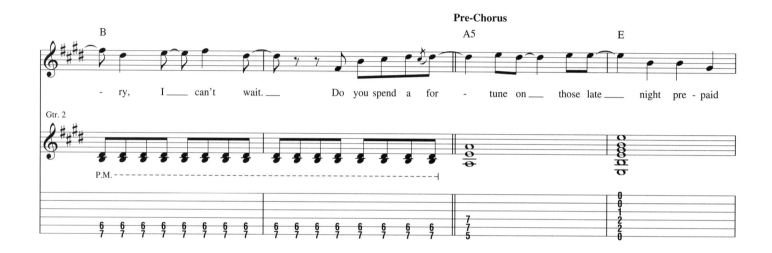

-ry, I __ can't wait. __   Do you spend a for - tune on __ those late __ night pre-paid

Gtr. 2

P.M. -

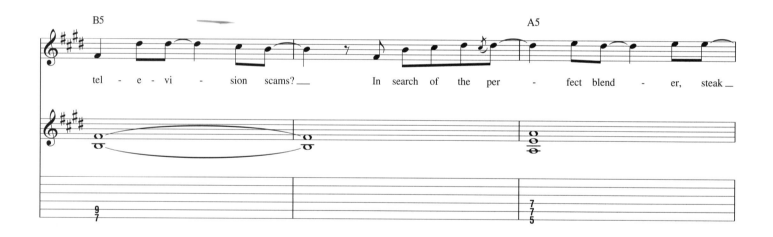

tel - e - vi - sion scams? __   In search of the per - fect blend - er, steak __

D.S. al Coda 1

__ knife and __ non-stick fry - ing pan? __   What if it was you? __

Gtrs. 2 & 3

P.M. - - - - - - - - - - - - -

Coda 1

Bridge

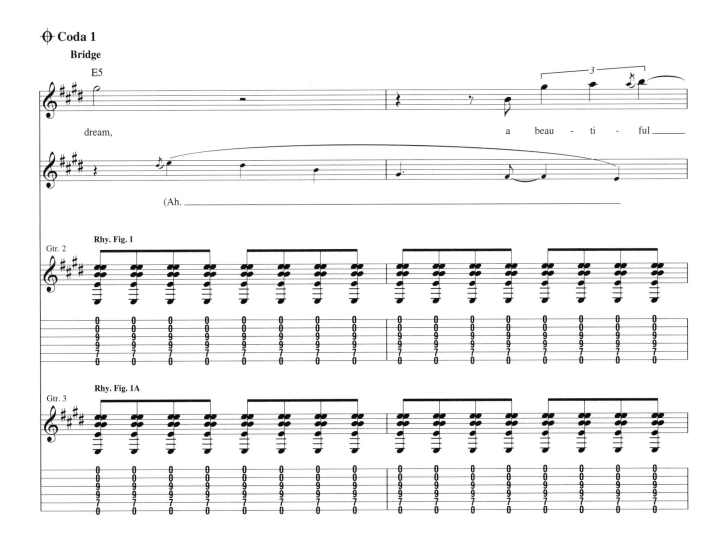

dream,

a beau - ti - ful _____

(Ah. _____

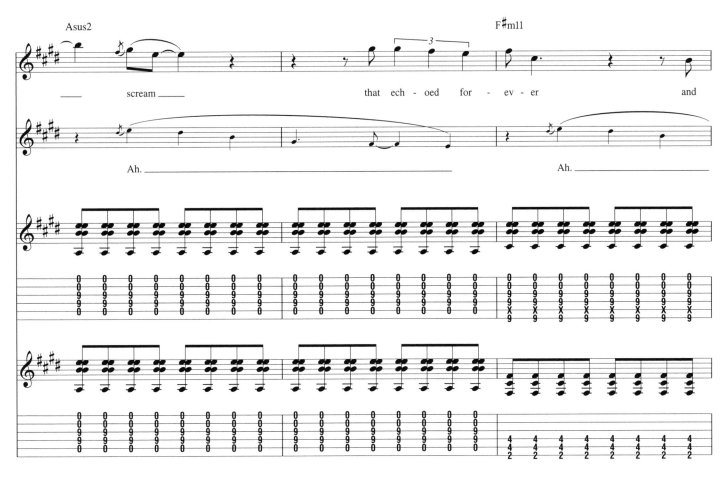

_____ scream _____

that ech - oed for - ev - er

and

Ah. _____

Ah. _____

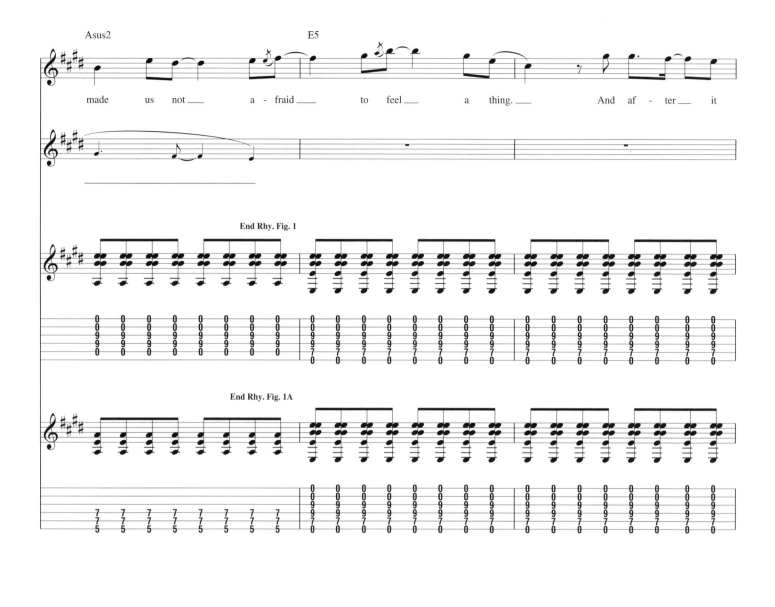

made   us   not ___   a - fraid ___   to   feel ___   a   thing. ___   And   af - ter ___   it

End Rhy. Fig. 1

End Rhy. Fig. 1A

Gtrs. 2 & 3: w/ Rhy. Figs. 1 & 1A (1st 6 meas.)

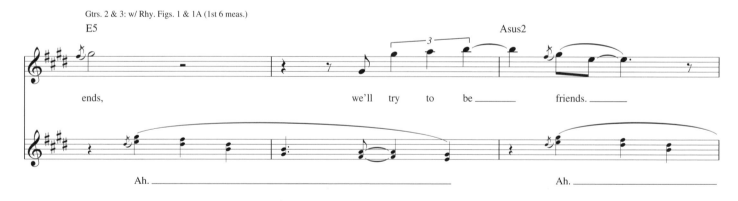

ends,   we'll   try   to   be ___   friends. ___

Ah. _____   Ah. _____

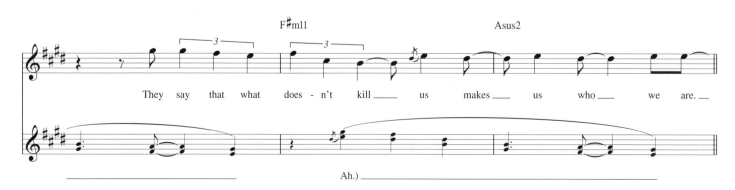

They   say   that   what   does - n't   kill ___   us   makes ___   us   who ___   we   are. ___

_____   Ah.) _____

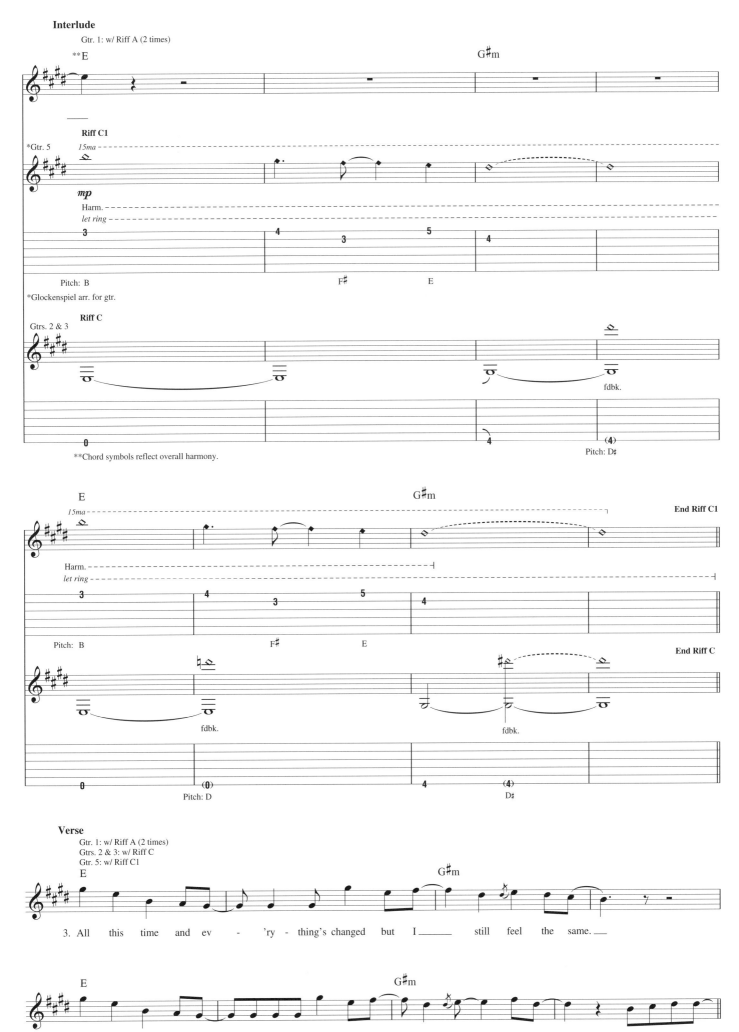

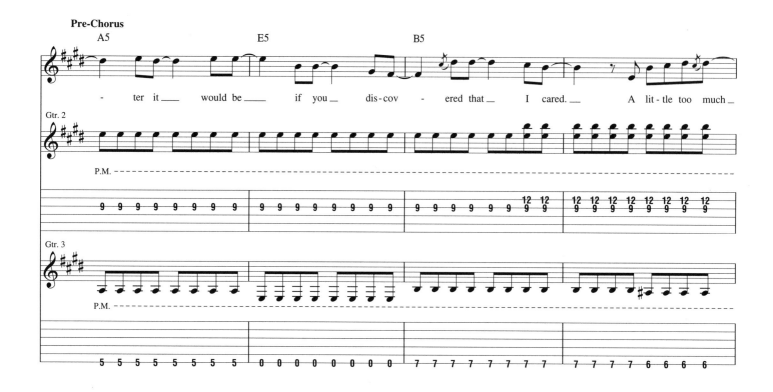

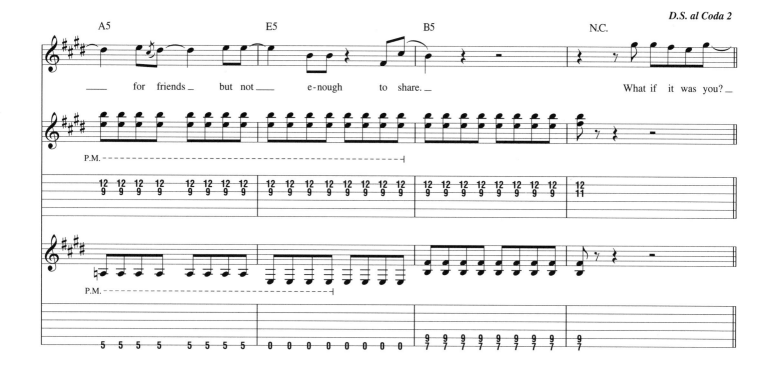

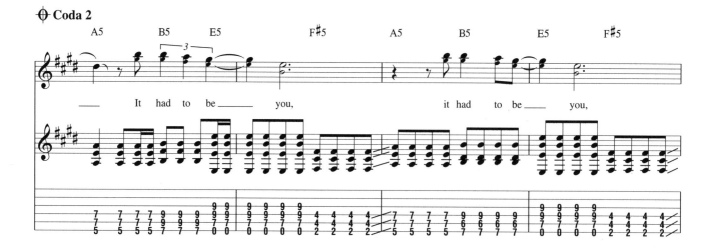

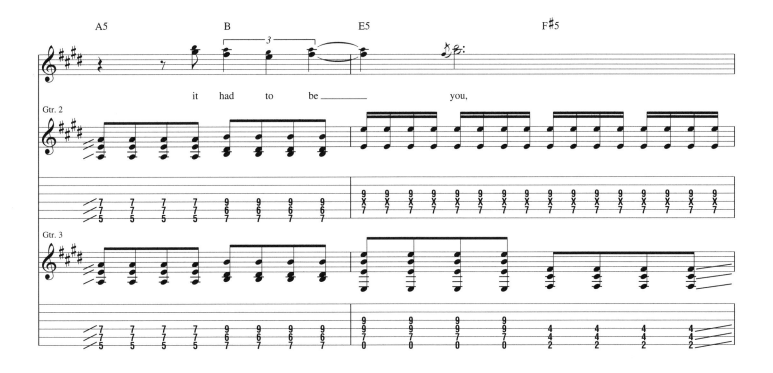

it had to be _____ you,

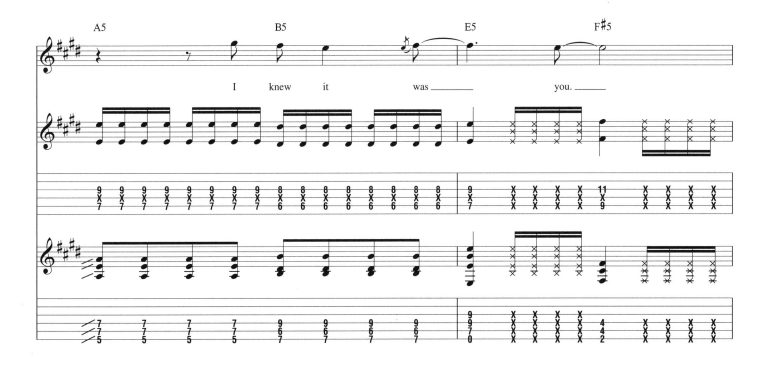

I knew it was _____ you. _____

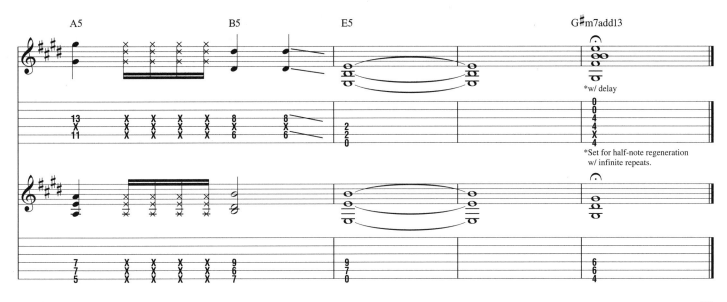

*w/ delay

*Set for half-note regeneration
w/ infinite repeats.

from *Even If It Kills Me*

Last Night

Words and Music by Justin Pierre, Joshua Cain, Jesse Johnson, Matthew Taylor and Tony Thaxton

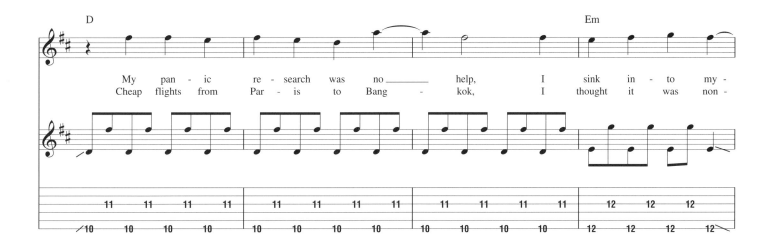

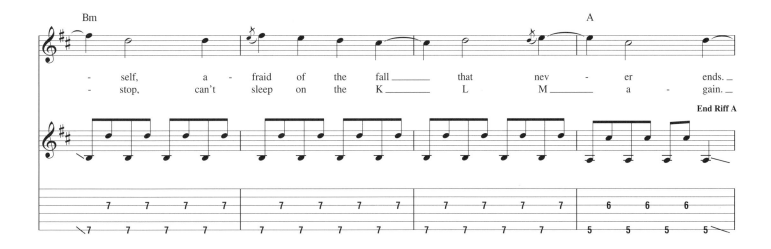

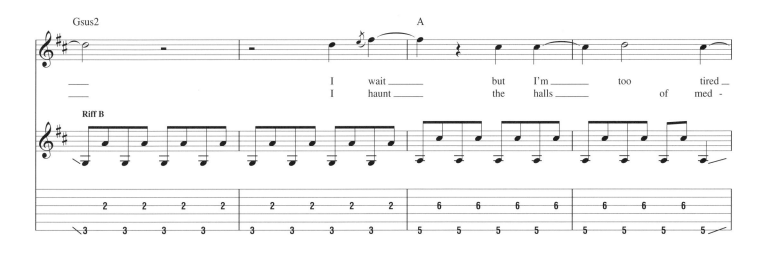

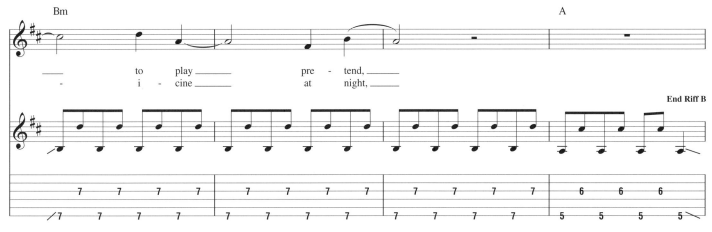

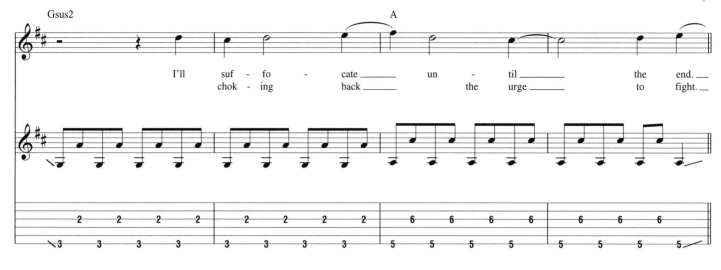

Gsus2

I'll suf - fo - cate _____ un - til _____ the end. _____
chok - ing back _____ the urge _____ to fight. _____

Interlude

Gtr. 1: w/ Riff A

Gtr. 2 (clean)

mp
w/ heavy reverb

let ring -
*T

*T=Thumb on 6th string

let ring -

(5)

D.S. al Coda

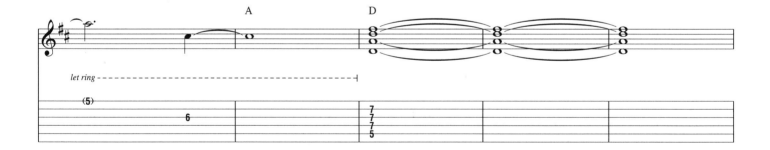

let ring -
T

⊕ Coda

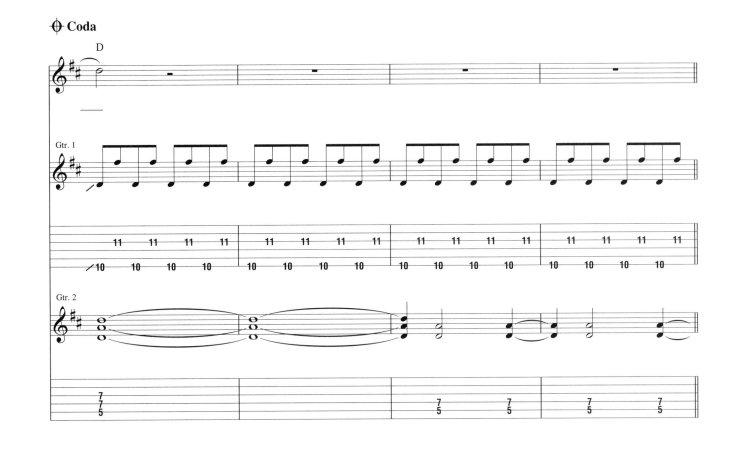

Verse

Gtr. 1: w/ Riff A

3. Her cat was claw - ing the floor - boards just out - side of our ____ door, the

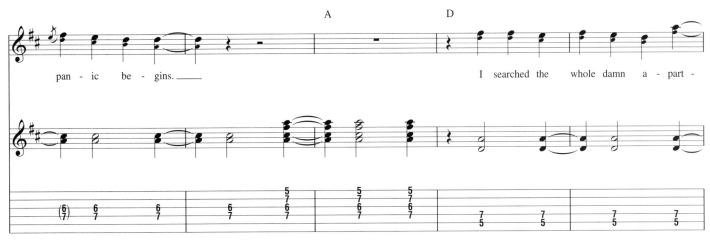

pan - ic be - gins. ____   I searched the whole damn a - part -

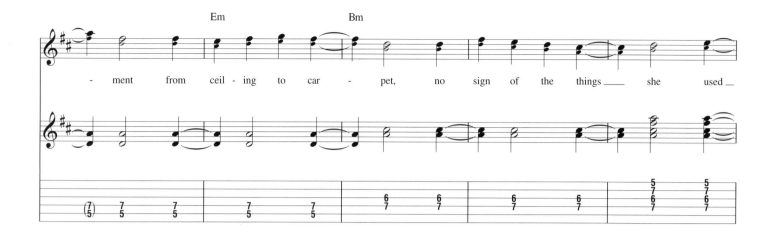

Gtr. 1: w/ Riff B (1 1/2 times)

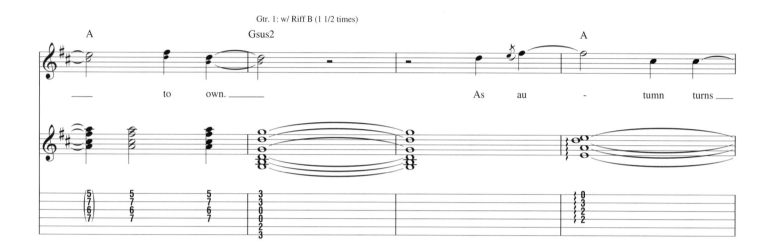

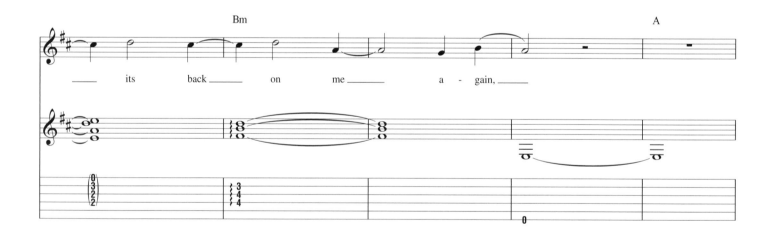

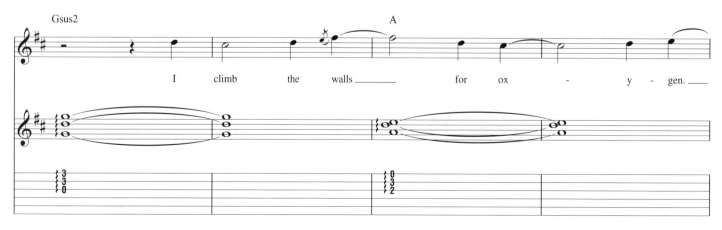

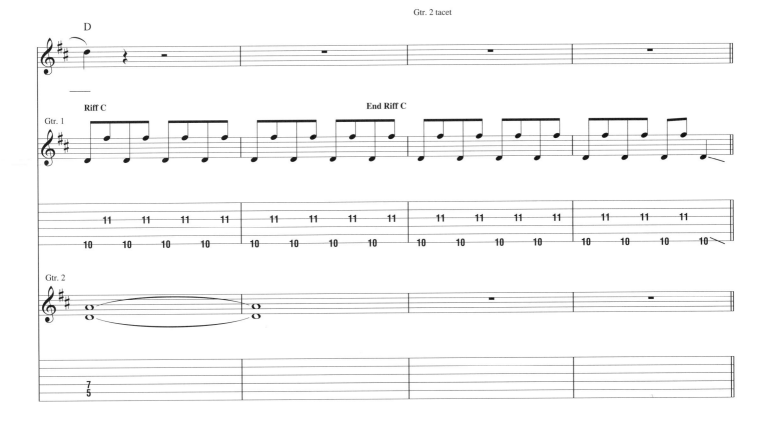

I trail her close - ly from be - hind, she tries hard not to ____

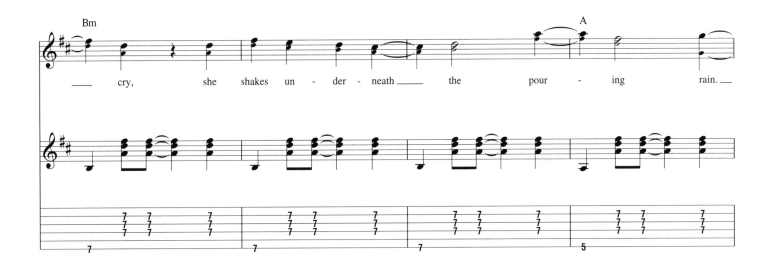

____ cry, she shakes un - der - neath ____ the pour - ing rain. ____

Gtr. 1: w/ Riff B (3 1/2 times)

I can't ____ com - pete ____ with all ____

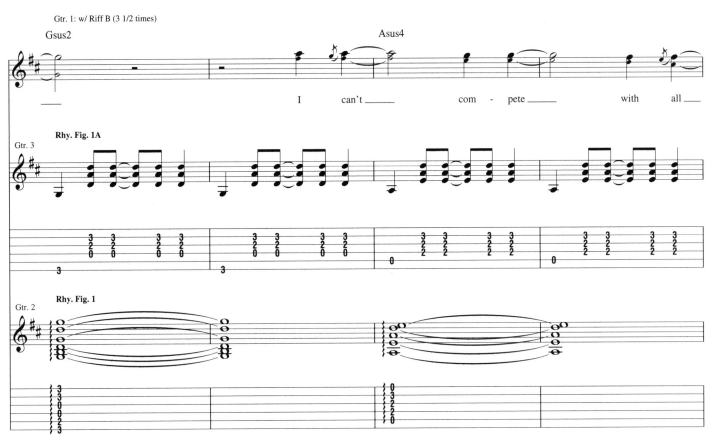

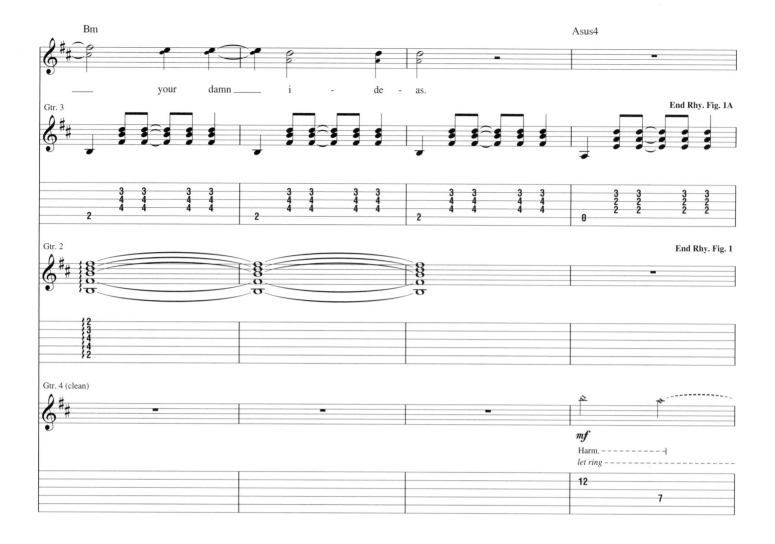

your damn   i - de - as.

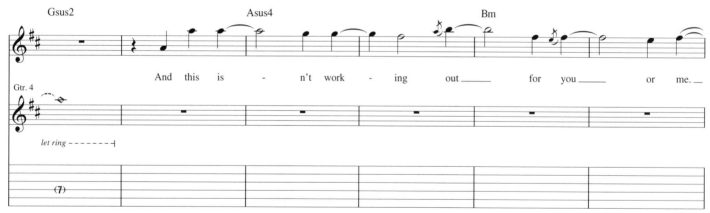

And this is - n't work - ing out ____ for you ____ or me. ____

The truth ____ is I'm ____ too tired ____

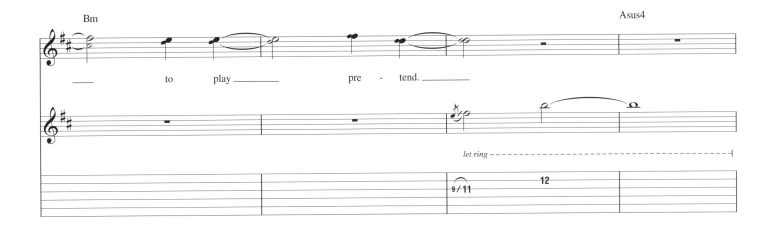

to play _____ pre - tend. _____

Gtr. 4 tacet

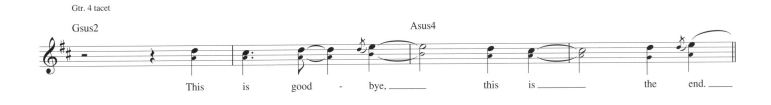

This is good - bye, _____ this is _____ the end. _____

Outro

Gtr. 1: w/ Riff C (3 1/2 times)

Gtr. 3

Gtr. 1: w/ Fill 1

Fill 1

Gtr. 1

from *Commit This to Memory*

Make Out Kids

Words and Music by Justin Pierre, Joshua Cain, Jesse Johnson, Matthew Taylor and Tony Thaxton

Tune down 1/2 step:
(low to high) E♭-A♭-D♭-G♭-B♭-E♭

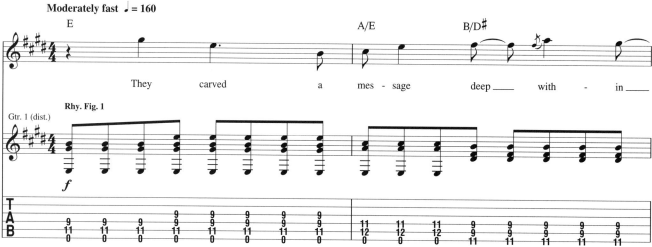

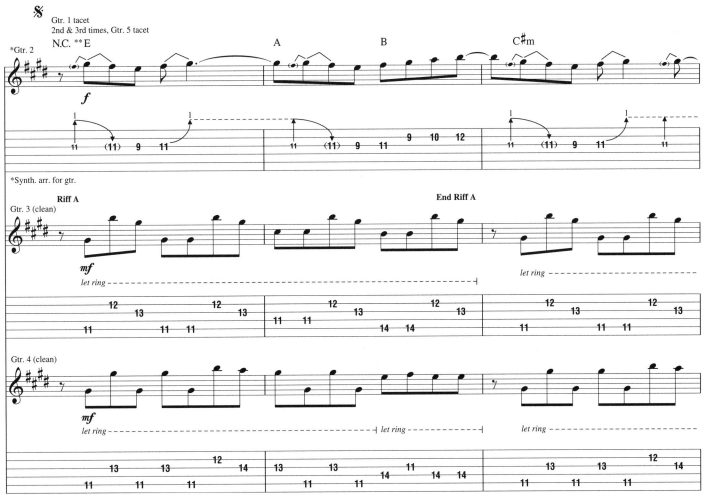

Riff A

End Riff A

*Synth. arr. for gtr.

**Chord symbols reflect overall harmony.

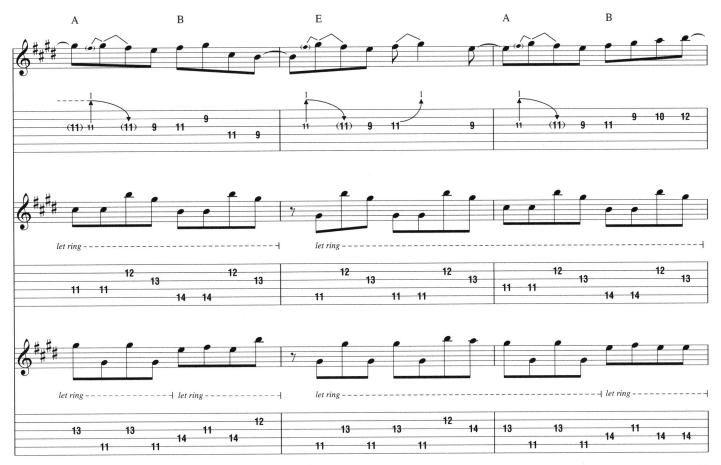

*Chord symbols implied by bass, next 8 meas.

math   and   mag   - a   - zines, ___   di - rec - tor's   cuts   and   gray ___ cell   green,
o - ver   win   - ter   break,   cock - tails   and   min - ia   - ture ___   mis - takes,
keep   in   touch ___   these   days, ___   I'm   liq - uid   cold, ___   she's   mur - der   grey,

To Coda 1

To Coda 2

armed   with   an   eye ___   for con   - tra - dic - tions,   she sees   com - plete - ly   through ___ me.
lights   out,   we're   cov - ered   in ___   each   oth - er's   warm ___ em - brace. ___   (And ___   we sing.)
hol - lowed   by   cir - cum - stance   that   pushed   us   both ___   a - way.

let's hope we nev-er have to _____ say good - bye, _____

D.S. al Coda 1

_____ say good - bye. _____

End Rhy. Fig. 2A

End Rhy. Fig. 2

$\oplus$ **Coda 1**

Chorus

Gtrs. 1 & 5: w/ Rhy. Figs. 2 & 2A

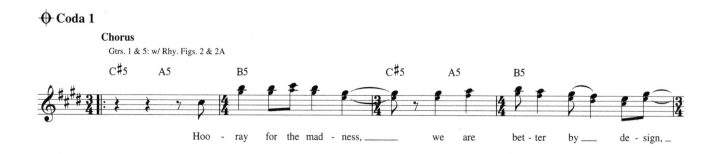

Hoo - ray for the mad - ness, _____ we are bet - ter by ___ de - sign,

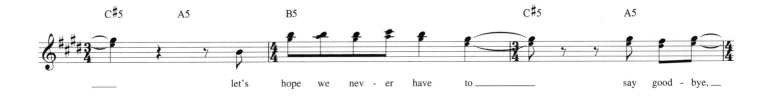

let's hope we nev - er have to ___ say good - bye,

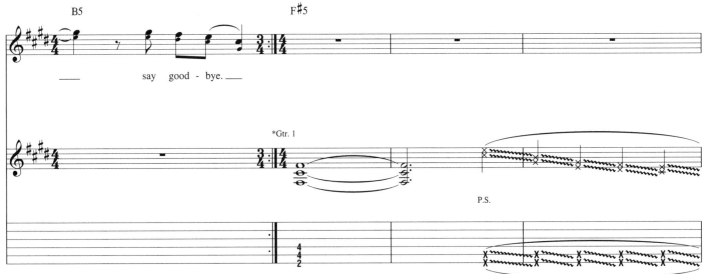

say good - bye. ___

*Gtr. 1

P.S.

*Doubled, next 8 meas.

Bridge

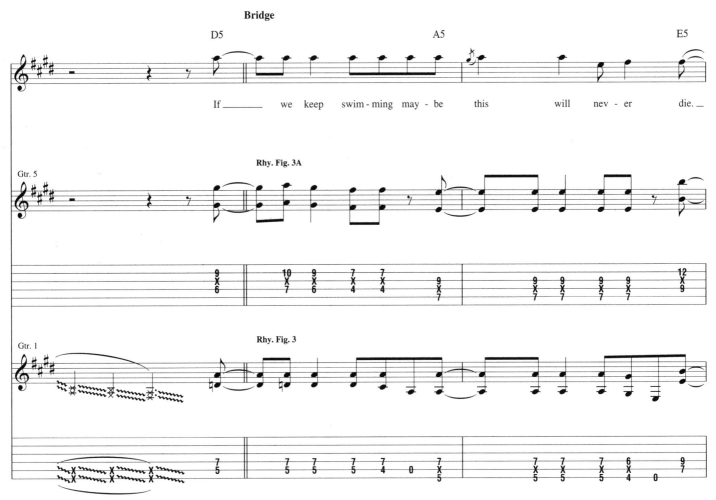

If ___ we keep swim - ming may - be this will nev - er die. ___

Rhy. Fig. 3A

Gtr. 5

Rhy. Fig. 3

Gtr. 1

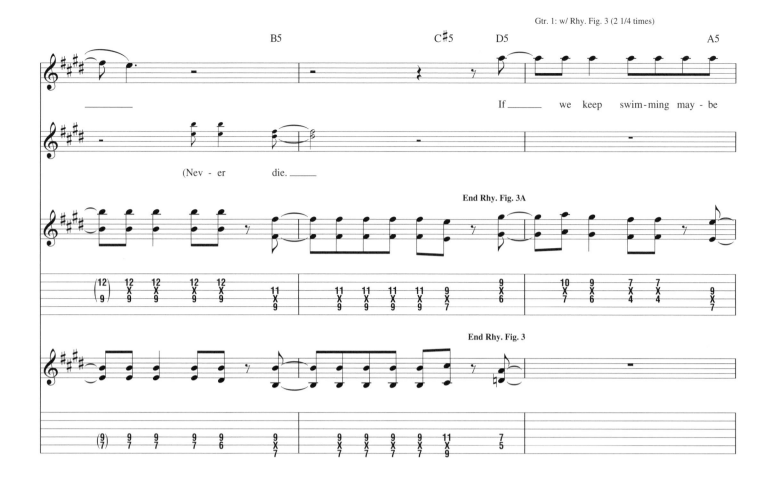

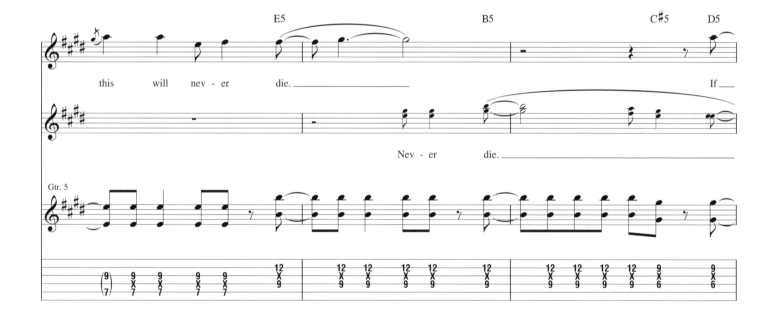

My Favorite Accident

Words and Music by Justin Pierre, Joshua Cain, Jesse Johnson, Matthew Taylor and Tony Thaxton

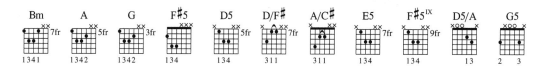

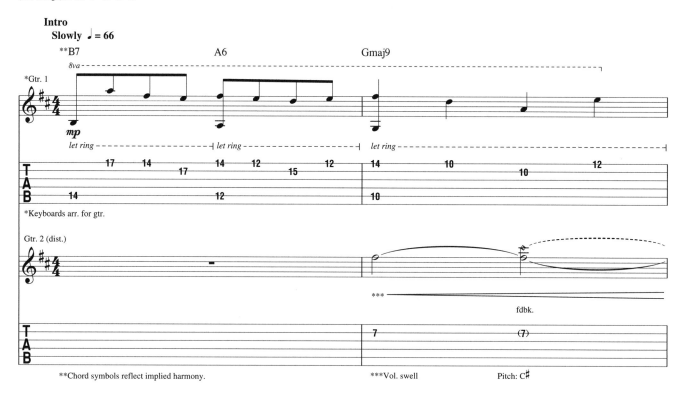

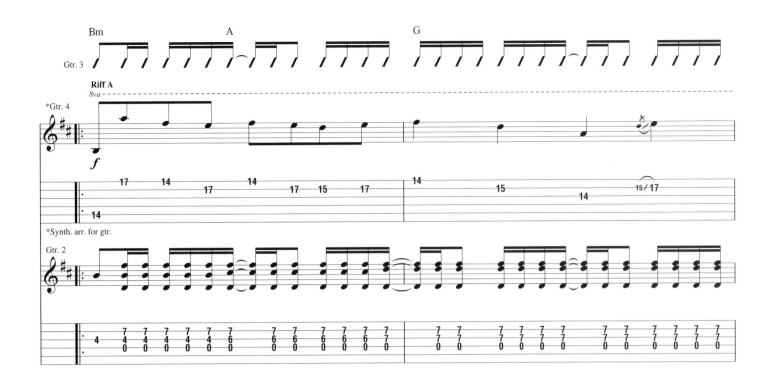

1. I got the mes-sage long be-fore _____ you said you ___ knew there was no chance of us ___ at all. ___

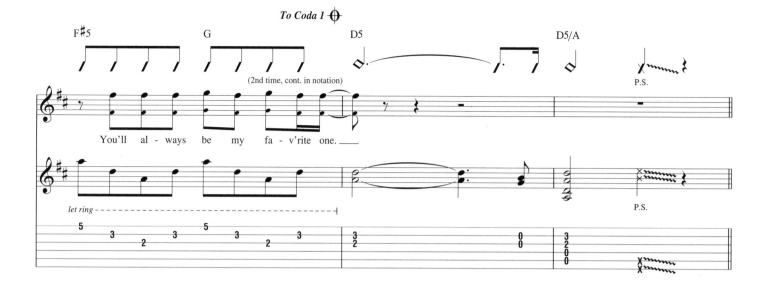

You'll al - ways be my fa - v'rite one. ___

Interlude

Gtr. 4: w/ Riff A

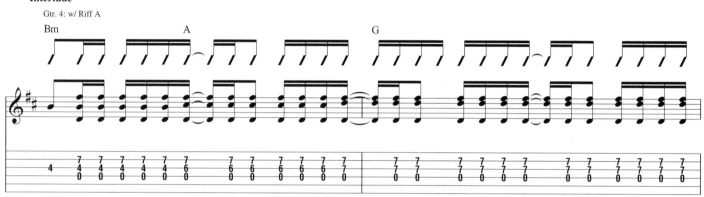

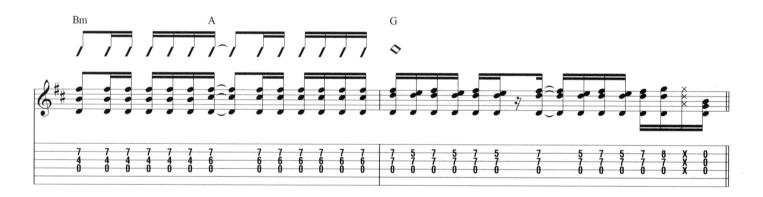

Verse
Double-time feel

2nd time, Gtr. 5 tacet

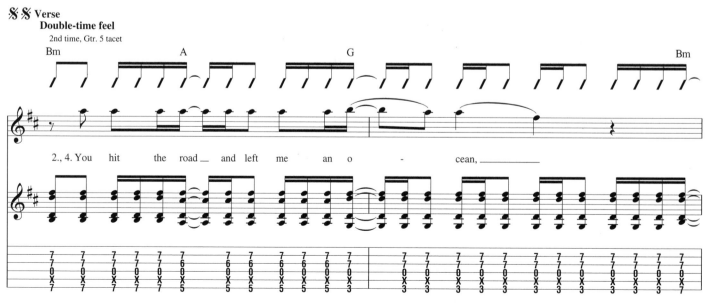

2., 4. You hit the road ___ and left me an o - ___ cean, ___

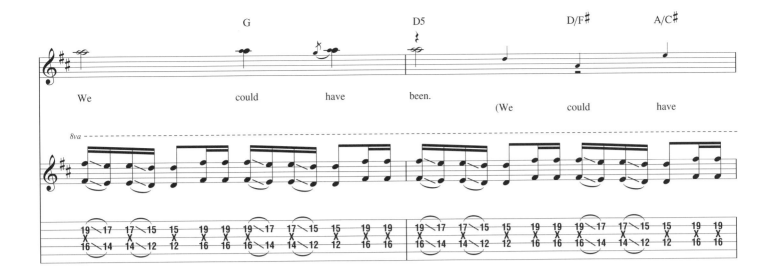

We could have been. (We could have

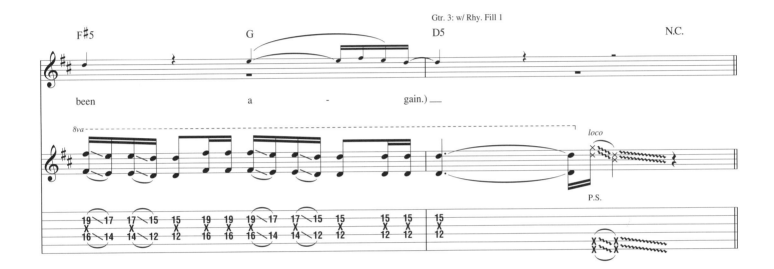

been a - gain.) —

Verse

Gtr. 2 tacet

3. Long wind - ed prom - is - es — of fu - ture com - pa - ny

Gtr. 5 (slight dist.)

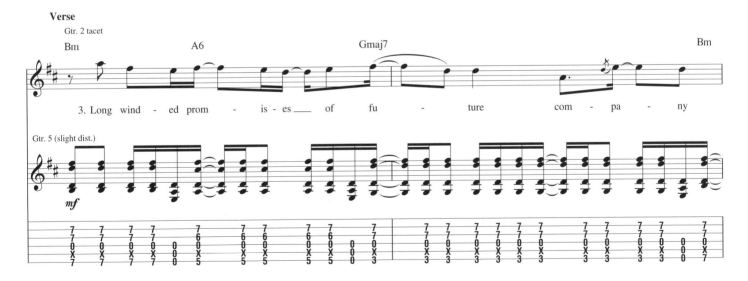

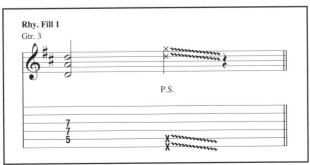

Rhy. Fill 1
Gtr. 3

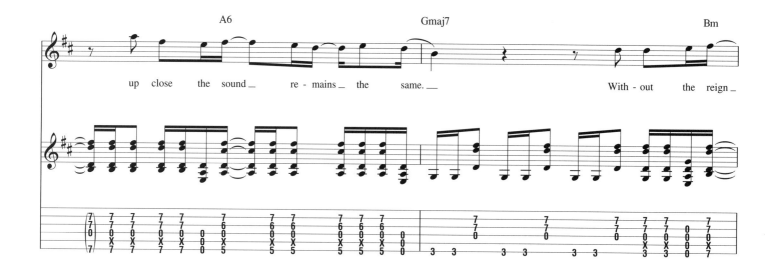

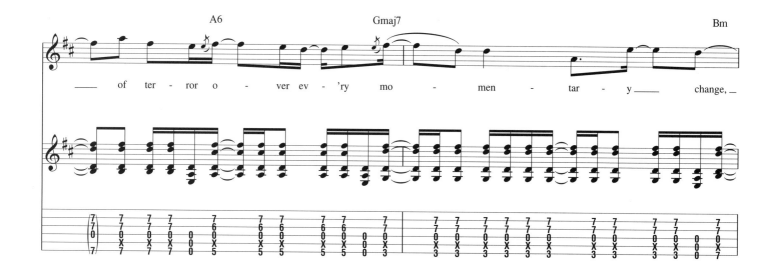

D.S.S. al Coda 2

*Composite arrangement

⊕ Coda 2

Outro

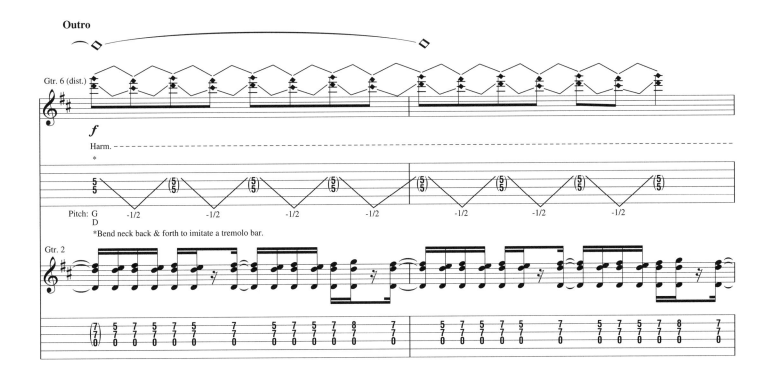

*Bend neck back & forth to imitate a tremolo bar.

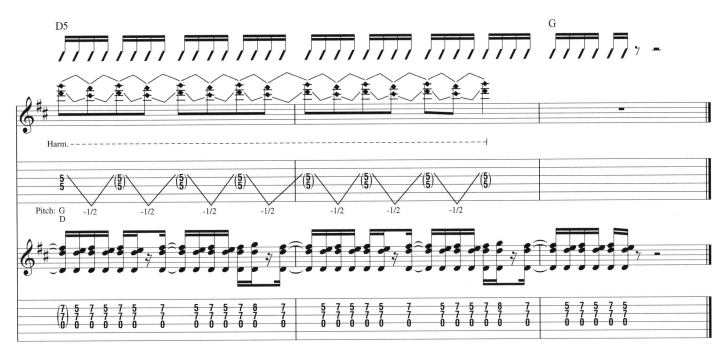

This Is For Real

Words and Music by Justin Pierre, Joshua Cain, Jesse Johnson, Matthew Taylor and Tony Thaxton

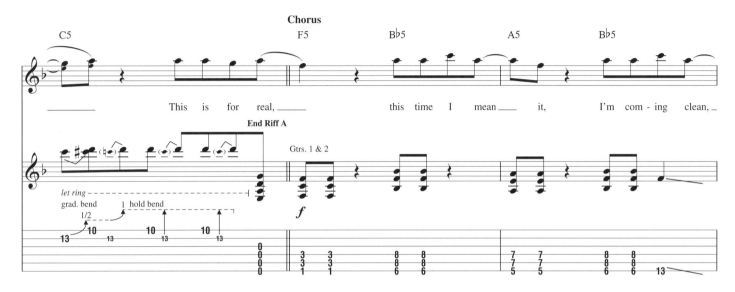

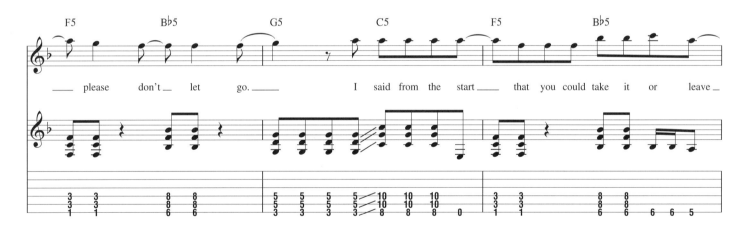

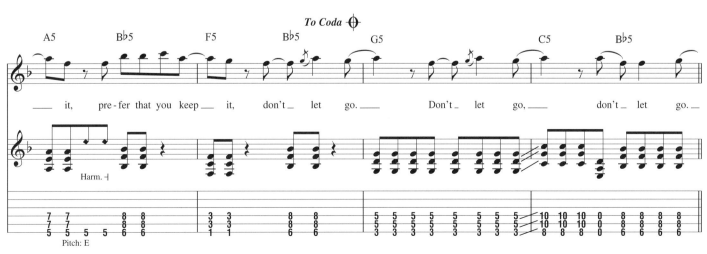

Interlude

*Chord symbols reflect overall harmony.

Coda

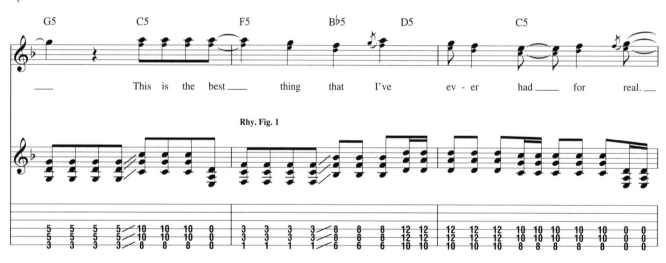

This is the best ___ thing that I've ev - er had ___ for real.

Rhy. Fig. 1

This is the best ___ thing that I've ev - er had ___ for real. ___

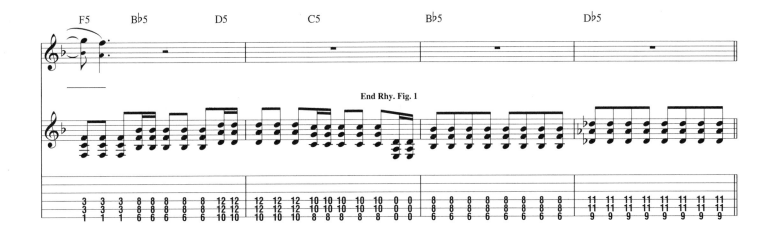

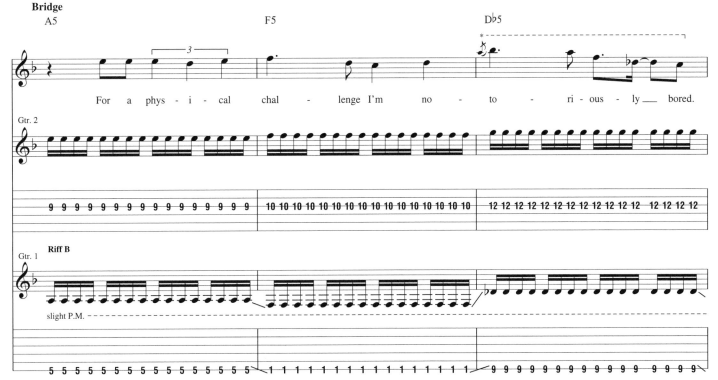

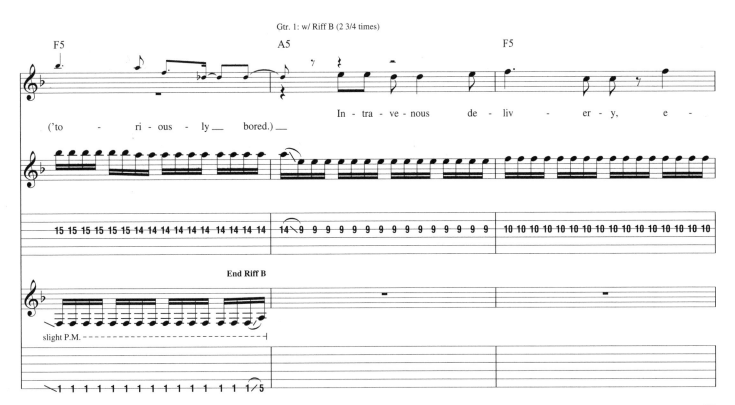

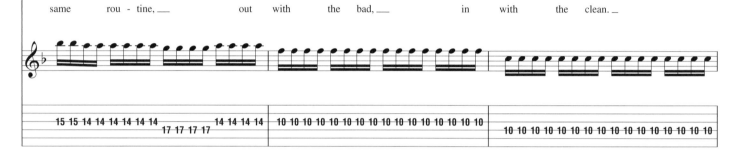

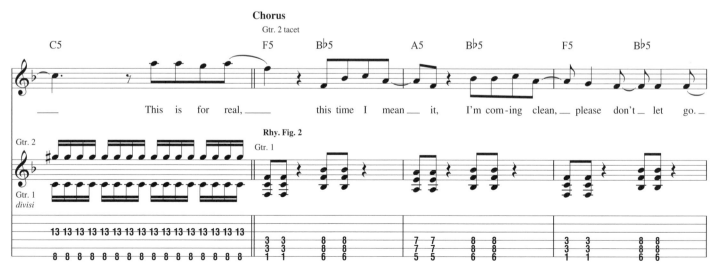

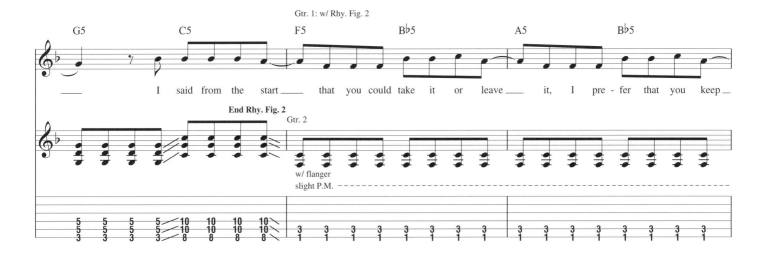

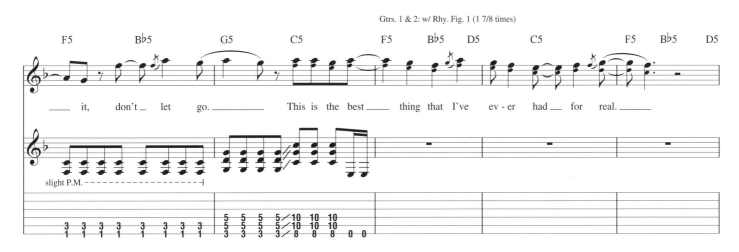

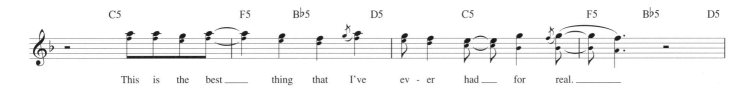

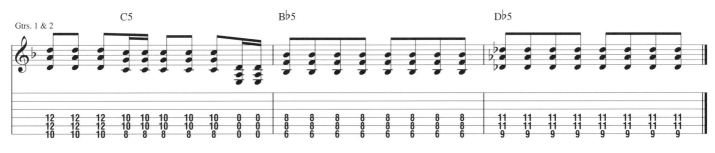

from *Commit This to Memory*

Time Turned Fragile

Words and Music by Justin Pierre, Joshua Cain, Jesse Johnson, Matthew Taylor and Tony Thaxton

Tune down 1/2 step:
(low to high) E♭-A♭-D♭-G♭-B♭-E♭

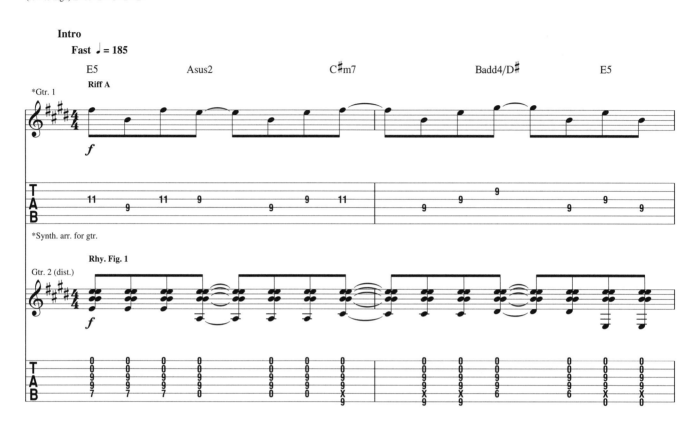

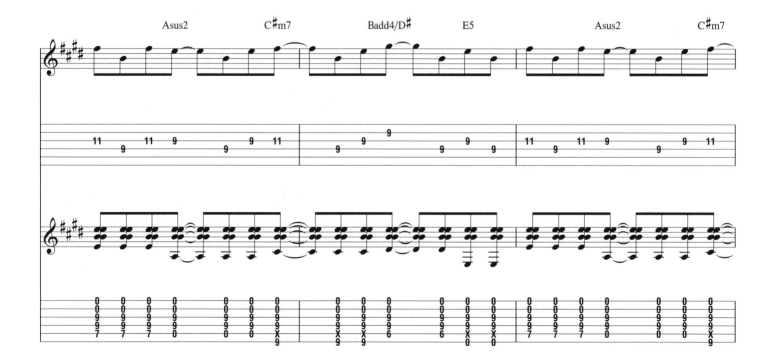

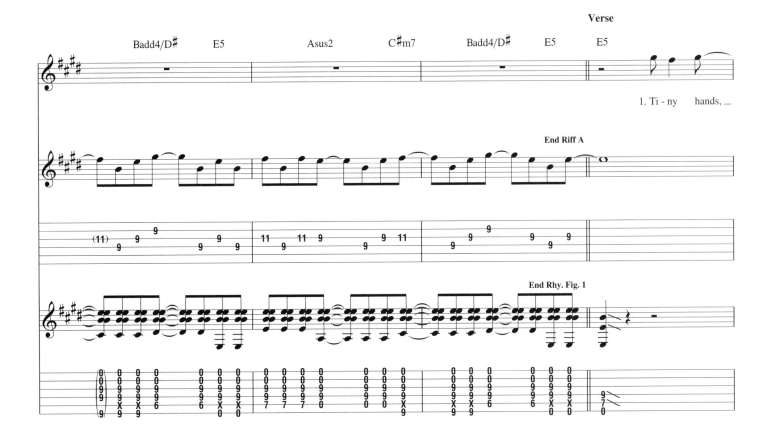

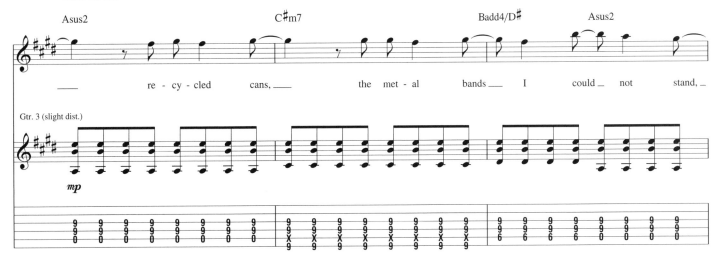

89

Interlude

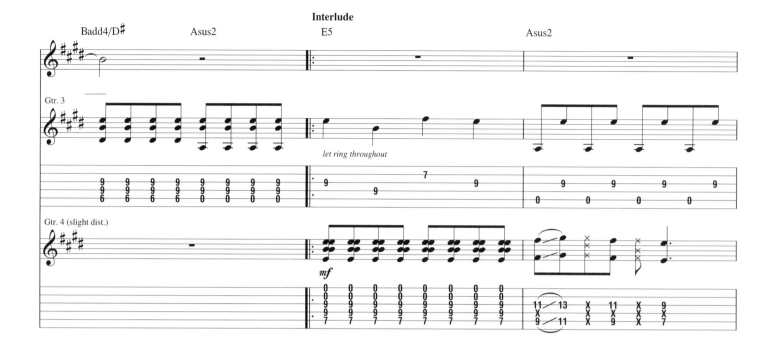

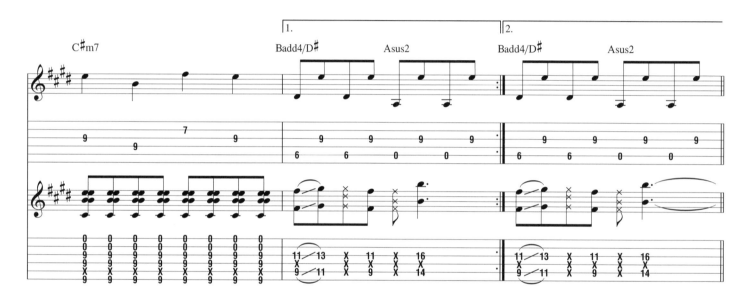

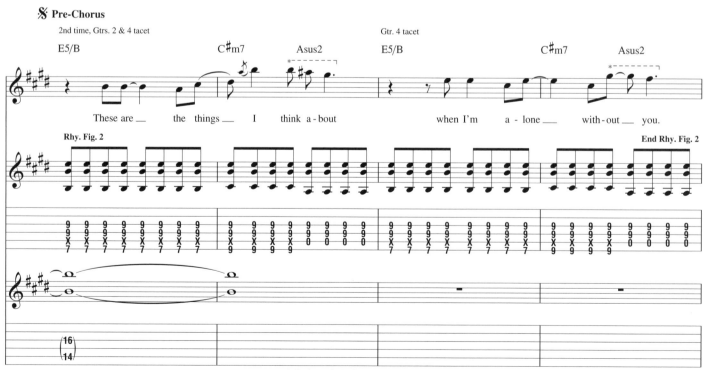

*w/ echo set for half-note regeneration w/ 1 repeat.

Coda 1

Bridge

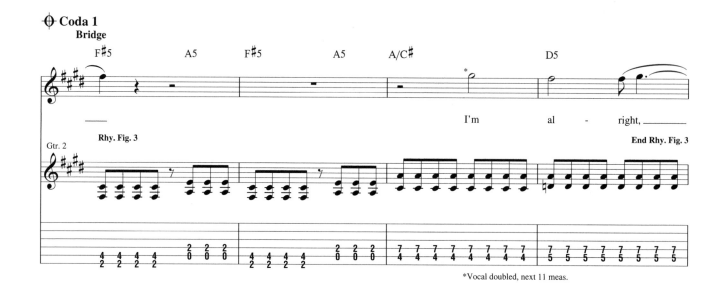

*Vocal doubled, next 11 meas.

Gtr. 2: w/ Rhy. Fig. 3 (2 times)

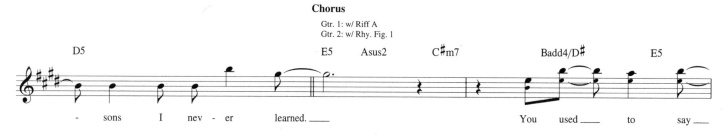

Chorus

Gtr. 1: w/ Riff A
Gtr. 2: w/ Rhy. Fig. 1

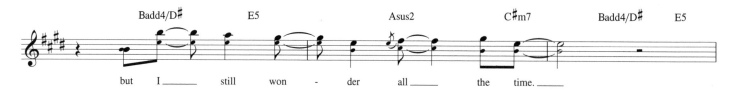

Bridge

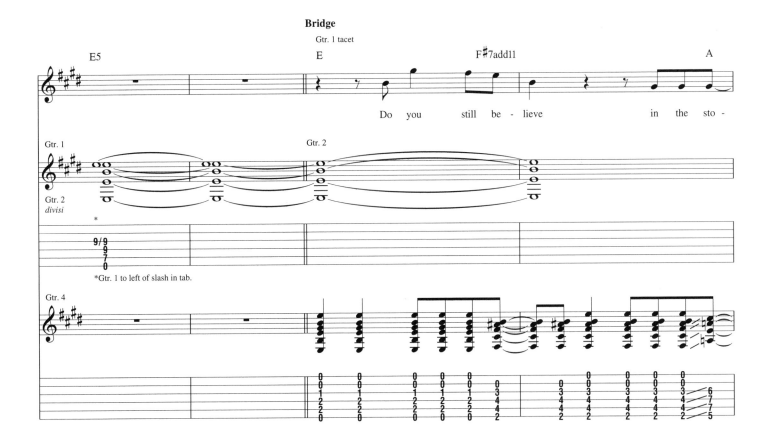

Do you still be - lieve in the sto -

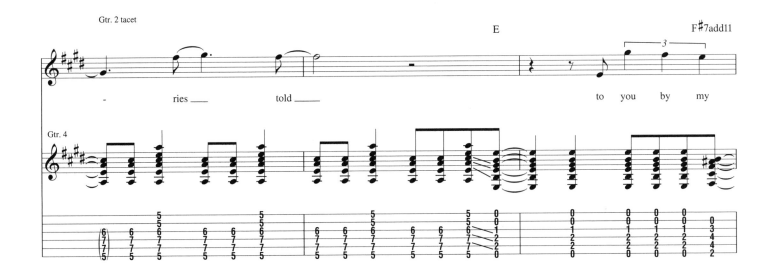

- ries ____ told ____   to you by my

friends and I ____ when you were four ____ years old? ____ How it

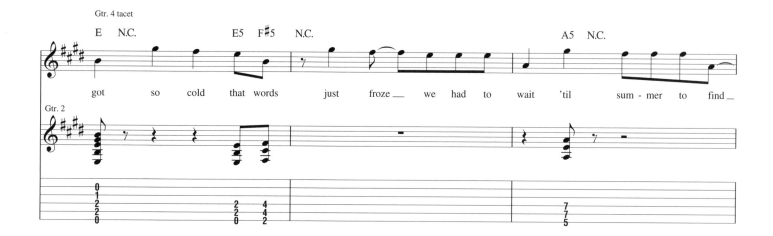

got   so   cold   that words   just   froze ___   we   had   to   wait   'til   sum - mer   to   find ___

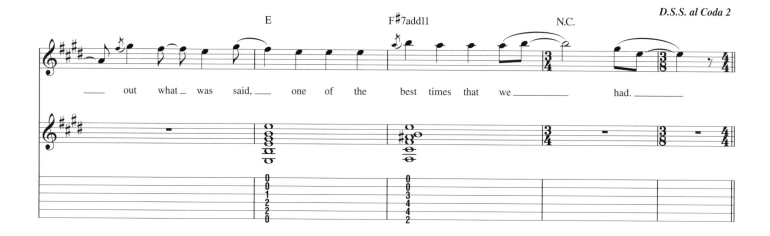

___   out   what ___ was   said, ___   one   of   the   best   times   that   we _____   had. _____

D.S.S. al Coda 2

⊕ Coda 2

Interlude

A

Riff B

End Riff B

w/ fingers

94

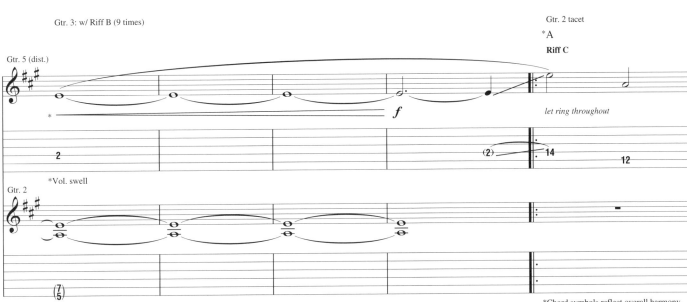

Gtr. 3: w/ Riff B (9 times)

Gtr. 5 (dist.)

Gtr. 2 tacet

*A

Riff C

let ring throughout

*Vol. swell

Gtr. 2

*Chord symbols reflect overall harmony.

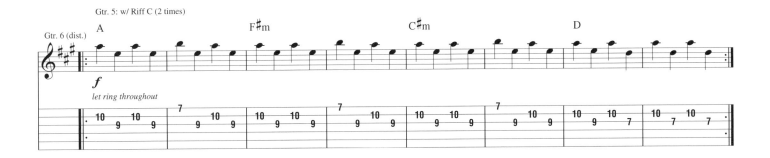

Gtr. 5

F#m

C#m

D

End Riff C

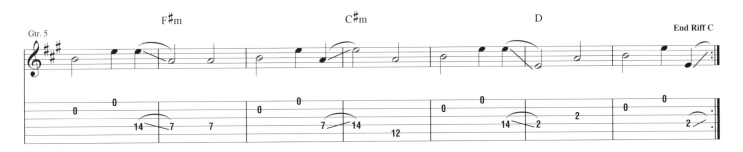

Gtr. 5: w/ Riff C (2 times)

Gtr. 6 (dist.)

A

F#m

C#m

D

let ring throughout

Outro

A

Gtr. 6 tacet

F#m

I was ner-vous from __ the start __ that our mus-cles might __ tear us

Gtr. 5

Riff D

w/ heavy reverb

Gtr. 6

**w/ echo set for half-note regeneration w/ 1 repeat, next 29 meas., lead voc. only.

a - part.

(Are mus-cles tear - ing us a - part?)

Gtr. 5

End Riff D

Gtr. 5: w/ Riff D (3 times)

A

F#m

From the words that carve _ our lives ___ to the words that take _ us by _

C#m

D

___ sur - prise.

(I was nev - er tak - en by ___ sur - prise.)

A

F#m

From the sounds that dis - ap - pear ___ to the chang - es we ___ be - gin _

C#m

D

A

___ to fear.

(I can hear you clear - ly.)

One

F#m

C#m

day I'll fail ___ to breathe ___ and all you'll have ___ are mem - o - ries.

*Gtr. 5: w/ Riff D (2 times)

D

16

(All we have ___ are mem - o - ries.) ___

*w/ delay and heavy reverb

from *Commit This to Memory*

When You're Around

Words and Music by Justin Pierre, Joshua Cain, Jesse Johnson, Matthew Taylor and Tony Thaxton

Drop D tuning, down 1/2 step:
(low to high) D♭-A♭-D♭-G♭-B♭-E♭

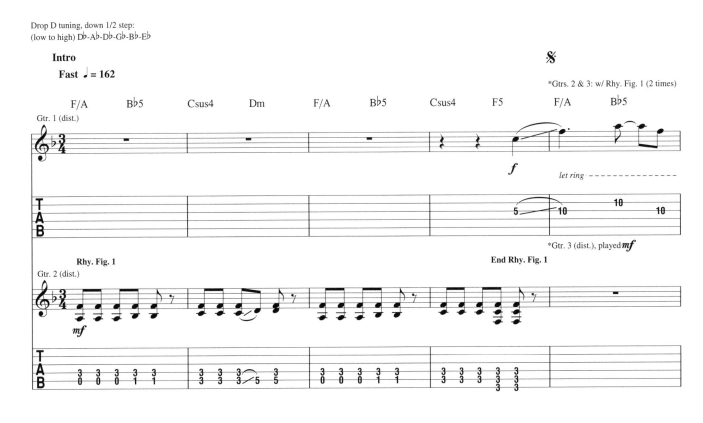

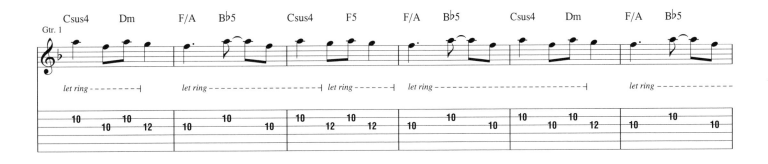

Verse

1. Mid - west love af - fair, __ I bend when I __ am bored.
2. Mid - west af - ter - math, __ the ru - mors start __ to rise. __

Riff A

Gtrs. 2 & 3

End Riff A

**Chord symbols reflect implied harmony.

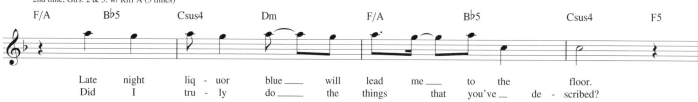

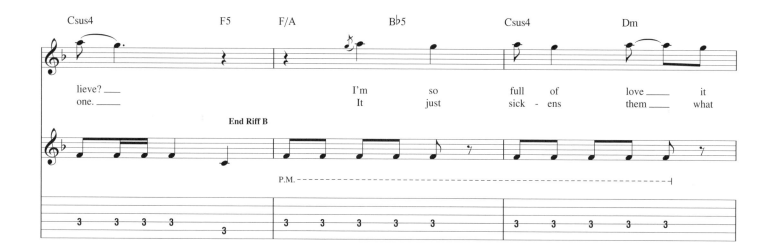

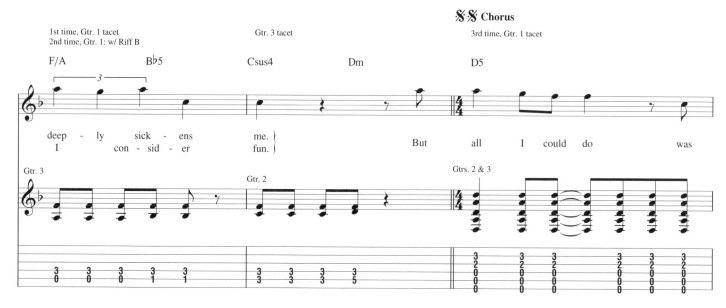

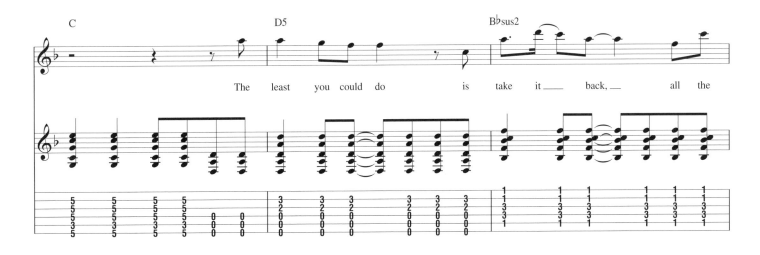

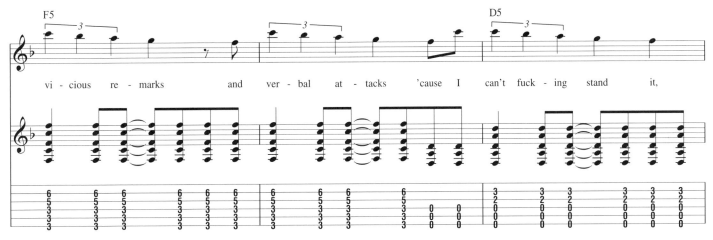

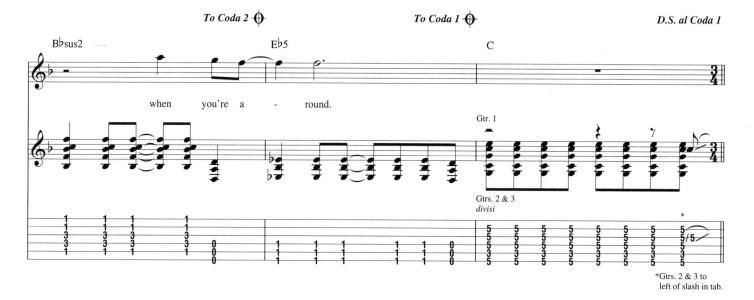

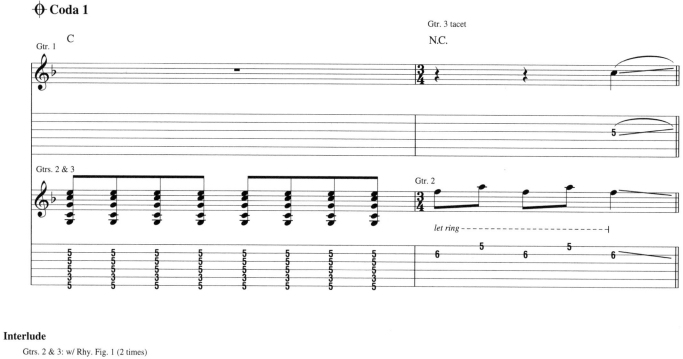

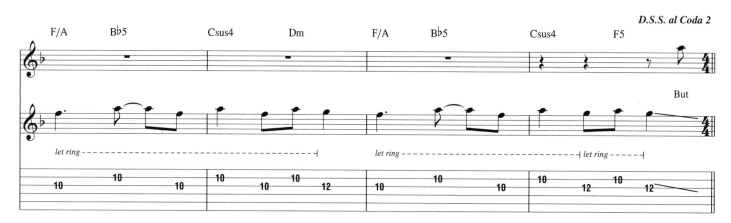

100

Coda 2

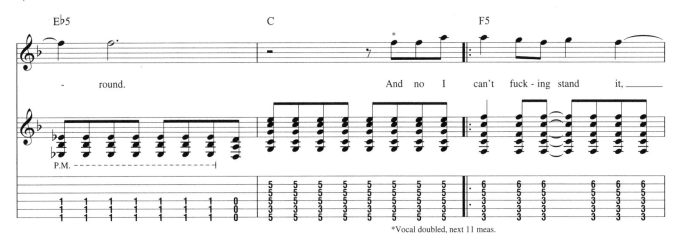

Vocal doubled, next 11 meas.

round. And no I can't fuck-ing stand it, _____

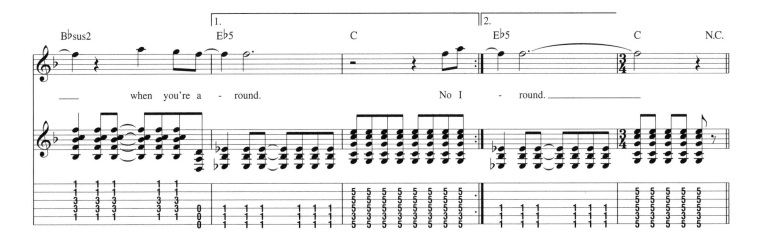

when you're a-round. No I _____ round. _____

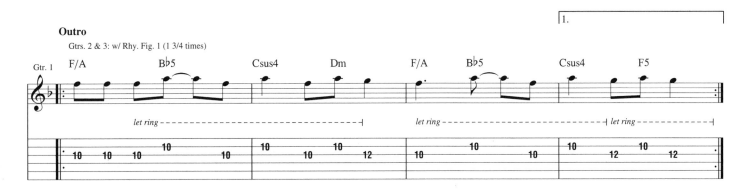

Outro

Gtrs. 2 & 3: w/ Rhy. Fig. 1 (1 3/4 times)

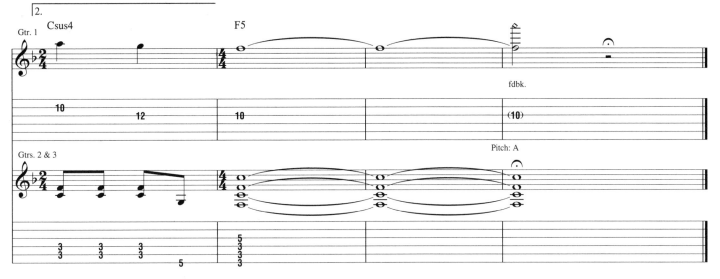

Guitar Notation Legend

Guitar music can be notated three different ways: on a *musical staff*, in *tablature*, and in *rhythm slashes*.

RHYTHM SLASHES are written above the staff. Strum chords in the rhythm indicated. Use the chord diagrams found at the top of the first page of the transcription for the appropriate chord voicings. Round noteheads indicate single notes.

THE MUSICAL STAFF shows pitches and rhythms and is divided by bar lines into measures. Pitches are named after the first seven letters of the alphabet.

TABLATURE graphically represents the guitar fingerboard. Each horizontal line represents a string, and each number represents a fret.

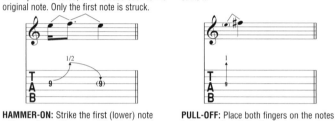

4th string, 2nd fret | 1st & 2nd strings open, played together | open D chord

HALF-STEP BEND: Strike the note and bend up 1/2 step.

WHOLE-STEP BEND: Strike the note and bend up one step.

GRACE NOTE BEND: Strike the note and immediately bend up as indicated.

SLIGHT (MICROTONE) BEND: Strike the note and bend up 1/4 step.

BEND AND RELEASE: Strike the note and bend up as indicated, then release back to the original note. Only the first note is struck.

PRE-BEND: Bend the note as indicated, then strike it.

VIBRATO: The string is vibrated by rapidly bending and releasing the note with the fretting hand.

WIDE VIBRATO: The pitch is varied to a greater degree by vibrating with the fretting hand.

HAMMER-ON: Strike the first (lower) note with one finger, then sound the higher note (on the same string) with another finger by fretting it without picking.

PULL-OFF: Place both fingers on the notes to be sounded. Strike the first note and without picking, pull the finger off to sound the second (lower) note.

LEGATO SLIDE: Strike the first note and then slide the same fret-hand finger up or down to the second note. The second note is not struck.

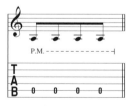

SHIFT SLIDE: Same as legato slide, except the second note is struck.

TRILL: Very rapidly alternate between the notes indicated by continuously hammering on and pulling off.

TAPPING: Hammer ("tap") the fret indicated with the pick-hand index or middle finger and pull off to the note fretted by the fret hand.

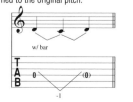

NATURAL HARMONIC: Strike the note while the fret-hand lightly touches the string directly over the fret indicated.

PINCH HARMONIC: The note is fretted normally and a harmonic is produced by adding the edge of the thumb or the tip of the index finger of the pick hand to the normal pick attack.

PICK SCRAPE: The edge of the pick is rubbed down (or up) the string, producing a scratchy sound.

MUFFLED STRINGS: A percussive sound is produced by laying the fret hand across the string(s) without depressing, and striking them with the pick hand.

PALM MUTING: The note is partially muted by the pick hand lightly touching the string(s) just before the bridge.

RAKE: Drag the pick across the strings indicated with a single motion.

TREMOLO PICKING: The note is picked as rapidly and continuously as possible.

VIBRATO BAR DIVE AND RETURN: The pitch of the note or chord is dropped a specified number of steps (in rhythm), then returned to the original pitch.

VIBRATO BAR SCOOP: Depress the bar just before striking the note, then quickly release the bar.

VIBRATO BAR DIP: Strike the note and then immediately drop a specified number of steps, then release back to the original pitch.

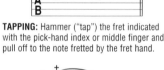